CHRIST IN THE STORM

KEEPING FAITH IN THE FACE OF THE UNKNOWN

DONNY ABBOTT

BLACK RIM PRESS, LLC

ISBN ebook: 978-1-7359223-2-4
ISBN paperback: 978-1-7359223-3-1
ISBN hardback: 978-1-73592223-4-8

Cover Art by:
Bethie Tel

Published by:
Donny Abbott
Black Rim Press, LLC
Fort Collins CO 80526
1

It is with my sincerest appreciation that I list the following authors, publishers and
titles of works I have quoted or referenced in this book, who have kindly granted
permission for their use, except where noted. All works belong to their respective
copyright owner(s), all rights reserved. These works are listed in random order.
Additional references are provided in the Notes section at the back of the book.

Dedicated in loving memory to my mom, Sylvia Abbott. My journey of faith began with you.

ACKNOWLEDGMENTS

Christ in the Storm has now been four years in the making. Many people have helped bring this project to life.

To my wife Shawna, along with your patience, you have generously given me the workspace and the support to become a writer. And to our three boys – Jack, Owen and Wyatt you make my life richer, and I am proud to be your dad.

Brent – I'm grateful for your friendship and for allowing me to sit in your office and talk about my lack of confidence on more than one occasion. Thank you for your theological brilliance and for your fidelity to Scripture. Many of the words in this book come from those office conversations.

Bethie – You have done it again! Creating a cover that is eye catching and offers the reader a chance to get a glimpse into what the book is about is a real gift. You have provided many of those gifts to me over the years.

Mary – You selflessly gave your time and literary skills to this project. Your passion for writing is evident as you helped me push this book to completion.

Joe – Your no-nonsense approach to editing helped me provide clarity and get to the point in what I was trying to write about.

Jennifer – With your thoughtfulness you led me to expand my writing and helped me gain a better understanding of how to write. Your insight into crafting words has made me a better author. Your understanding of Scripture has made me a better pastor. Your encouragement and belief in me has made me a better person.

Ricky, Clare, Hannah and Josh – I know during the darkest days of your storm you never thought you would see the cloud's part and the sun shine again. I hope you know you are an inspiration to many.

Rick and Susan – Your story is still unfolding yet you allow so many of us into your world to witness it. As role models for what it means to have faith in the storms of life, you are a blessing to us all.

Beta Readers – Brett, Dianne and Kiersten – I appreciate your critical eye and the time you've given to help put the final touches on this book.

To everyone mentioned above, please know that I feel the deepest gratitude for each of the unique ways you have helped me reach this milestone in my life, and I thank you from the bottom of my heart. I am indebted to each of the above people and to all who will read the words within these pages.

Finally a special thank you to **God** as the only One who is capable of calming all the storms in our lives, if we simply invite Him into our hearts.

Donny Abbott - July 2021

ALSO BY DONNY ABBOTT

Stanley the Claustrophobic Miner

Christ in the Storm

Facing the Lions*

*Forthcoming (2022)

CONTENTS

INTRODUCTION

Of the hundreds of paintings, etchings, and drawings that Dutch artist Rembrandt Harmenszoon van Rijn created, his "Christ in the Storm on the Sea of Galilee" is his only known seascape. This painting, one of several painted by Rembrandt in the early 1630s, was created in 1633. Born in Leiden, Netherlands, Rembrandt began to study art at the age of fourteen. As he approached mid-life, he moved to Amsterdam and was already an accomplished artist who had undoubtedly experienced various highs and lows throughout his artistic career.

This painting highlights the physical and spiritual struggles of living in our world—struggles that Rembrandt would come to know all too well when his wife and three of his four children would die within a seven-year period.

I first happened upon the painting as a teenager and was

immediately drawn to the peril the sailors were facing as they battled this fierce storm. So much emotion is coming through the brushstrokes of paint that I have literally spent hours over the course of my life contemplating this painting. The first thing that catches my eye is the white waves of the windswept sea raising the tiny boat high into the air.

There is a dichotomy between the sailors at the front half of the boat frantically fighting for their lives in the painted light, and the almost oblivious serenity of the men in the dark at the bottom half of the boat. This light and darkness provide contrast to the chaotic scene captured by the apostle Matthew in the gospel that bears his name.

The painting had been on display for over ninety years at the Isabella Stewart Gardner Museum in Boston, Massachusetts. Having been a collector of rare works of fine art, Gardner set about creating a museum that could house this painting along with other precious artifacts. She purchased the painting in 1898 to add to her collection of rare works of fine art. Her museum was completed in 1901, and to this day, over 200,000 people per year visit the museum that displays more than 7,500 paintings, sculptures, furniture, textiles, silver, ceramics, 1,500 rare books, and 7,000 archival objects from ancient Rome, Medieval Europe, Renaissance Italy, Asia, the Islamic world and nineteenth-century France and America.

Unfortunately, this rare Rembrandt hasn't been seen in public in over thirty years, as the Gardner is also home to the biggest unsolved art theft in modern history. At 1:24 a.m. on

March 18, 1990, security guard, Richard Abath, went to investigate a knocking at the employee entrance door. Two men were on the other side of the door who identified themselves as Boston police officers sent there to investigate reports of a disturbance. Abath, going against security protocol but feeling comfortable in their explanation, buzzed them in. Once inside they calmly asked Abath to come out from the counter he was standing behind and promptly informed him that there was a warrant out for his arrest. Abath, at the time, was a struggling musician and would occasionally smoke some marijuana. Perhaps he thought that the police had something on him about his pot-smoking past, so he went about obeying their orders. Once Abath was away from the counter, the police officers calmly proclaimed to Abath and his night-watch partner, "Gentlemen, this is a robbery."

Now away from the "panic" button behind the counter, Abath and his partner were at the mercy of their captors. They were led at gunpoint down to the basement where the "officers" tied them up and then spent the next eighty-one minutes pulling off a masterfully planned art heist. By 2:45 a.m., the thieves exited the building having stolen thirteen works of rare art by Degas, Vermeer, and Rembrandt. The total value for these stolen works of art was over $500 million. The thieves were methodical and knew exactly what they were looking for, specifically targeting Rembrandt's works located in the "Dutch Room." Amongst the works stolen was "Christ in the Storm on the Sea of Galilee" making this heist all the more disheartening.

As I mentioned, I have always loved this painting. There is so much chaos taking place in this scene. From the calmness on the right side of the boat to the frantic fight for survival on the other. The differences make for one of Rembrandt's most intriguing paintings.

I also love learning about Scripture through art as a way of gaining insight on a passage. Art has a way of bringing the passage to life in a very visual way. There is frequently an aura of mystery surrounding any great work of art. With most of these great works being hundreds of years old, the modern-day viewer is often left with questions about the artist, the scene painted, and dozens of other unanswered questions. The intrigue only grows with the passage of time, especially when you throw in an art heist or two; sinister tales adding to the mystery.

Although Rembrandt used much artistic license in his depiction of the Matthew 8 biblical passage, "Christ in the Storm on the Sea of Galilee" helps me understand what this event may have looked like when it took place. Other than text and long before movies and television were invented, art was a primary means of bringing a story to life. Meditating on a piece of artwork is known as Visio Divina (Divine Seeing). Like the practice of Lectio Divina, where a reader will re-read and pray over a text several times, Visio Divina is a discipline where a person takes their time praying over a work of art.

This practice involves pondering art so that a person might see how God is working in the story the artwork is depicting. An article I recently came across provides a great description of the practice[1]:

> "It's the idea of seeing God through that which is created and invites us to see deeply, beyond first and second impressions, below initial ideas, judgments or understandings. It invites us to be seen, addressed, surprised and transformed by God who is never limited or tied to any image, but speaks through them."

In this painting, you can immediately see the obvious: there are people in a boat fighting a fierce storm that seemingly came out of nowhere. If you take a minute to really look at the scene, you can almost feel what they are going through. You see determination, grit, and fear all within the confined space of a twenty-foot-long fishing boat. You get a sense that their struggle is similar to what we all face when calamity strikes. The sailors know that Jesus is in the boat, but He doesn't seem to be too concerned about what is happening. Perhaps He doesn't know there is trouble.

It can seem the same with us at times also. With the fast pace of the world in which we live, we are often left to wonder if anyone cares about the crisis we are facing. We might know intellectually Jesus is with us, but how does that explain the stress, worry, and fear we feel during the difficult times?

In the painting, the disciples express similar emotions to those we experience when confronted with uncertainty about the future. Some of the sailors look as if they are trying to solve this problem all on their own. Look closely and you will see the fishermen holding sails and ropes tight. If need be, we are determined to face our trials on our own, too. Part of this is pride, and part of it is self-sufficiency. There is also a side of us that doesn't want to be vulnerable or seem weak in admitting our need for others. Deep down, however, no one wants to go through struggles alone. At times, we are reluctant to look for help as we are not sure if help will come. And if it does come, will it be the right kind of help? Of course, the hope we cling to is that Jesus will come through for us in our darkest of times, bringing sense to a hopeless situation.

Notice the central focus to the biblical story and to this painting—Jesus. It's obvious there are two very distinct scenes being played out in the painting. There are five men at the top side of the boat doing what you would expect sailors to do in a storm—battening down the hatches, taking down the sails, holding on for dear life. It shouldn't be lost on any of us that those men, although working the hardest, are also the farthest in proximity to Jesus. I wonder if there is something to that.

On the bottom half of the scene, there are eight figures. They are closest to Jesus and the ones least involved with the storm. There seems to be very little struggle on their behalf, except for the sailor on the far right who is really struggling with the rudder. They are the ones least engaged with the storm but most engaged with Jesus. As I ponder this painting, I think of the psalmist who reminds us that God is "an ever-present help in times of trouble." I don't know about you, but oftentimes, I don't think God is ever-present or very helpful when I face troubles. That certainly seems to be the case in the painting as Jesus is obviously present but doesn't appear to be of much help. After all, He is semi-reclining and isn't particularly bothered by all that is going on around Him. We can feel the same way at times, can't we? That God isn't bothered when we face difficult life circumstances? And herein lies the tension we all face. What the disciples learned, and what we will discover on the other side of heaven, is that,

...Jesus *was* present in our troubles;

...He *was* in control;

...He *did* care;

...He *knew* what the outcome would be;

...He was right there *with us* all along.

Back to the painting. There is also comedy and realism presented in the painting as Rembrandt painted a guy with his head over the side of the boat; we all know what he's doing. The guy right above him is praying. There are two sailors close to Jesus, and I would suspect they are the angriest with Him for sleeping and for allowing them to venture into this terrible storm in the first place. To the left of the old man whose back is turned to us is a faint, hardly distinguishable figure. I don't know if you see what I see, but it looks like a figure that you can see through. You might call it a ghost, but I wonder if it could possibly be an angel. This angelic figure is standing in the middle of the fight and calm, the dark and light. Perhaps Rembrandt painted the angel in the middle of the two scenes to represent their ability to travel between the heavens and the Earth.

The lighting is also interesting as Rembrandt cast the men at the top half of the boat in light, whereas he painted those closest to Jesus on the bottom half in a darker hue. I wonder why? Shouldn't it be the other way around? If Jesus is the Light of the World, why would Rembrandt cast Him in the dark? Maybe Rembrandt wanted to remind us that Jesus is with us in a dark world? We hope to find answers to all these questions.

"Christ in the Storm on the Sea of Galilee" sets the stage for the rest of this book—a book about keeping faith in the face of the unknown. It is also, to a certain extent, a book about dealing with fear. One thing I have learned in my fifty plus years of living is that you really can't have one without the other. What tends to happen in life is that we are good at having the one—fear—and not so good at having the other —faith.

Fear is universal, isn't it? Every person on Earth has some sort of fear that causes varying degrees of anxiety. But not everyone has faith. Some fears are good, as they warn us against things we should be respectful of, like snakes, fire or angry mothers of any sort. Other fears are more of what we deal with every day—the fear of losing a child to drugs or death. The fear of losing a job. Or, as in the case of my friends Ricky and Clare, both are living with fear of the unknown. Recently, Clare's dad was diagnosed with cancer. A few months later her ten-year-old daughter was diagnosed with leukemia.

While both are fighting these cancers, the outcome is uncertain and there is a great deal of fear in their lives. Other fears are not so rational and can be quite debilitating, such as the fear of going outside, of germs or nyctophobia (fear of the night). No matter what fear we each may battle, trying to overcome that particular fear is a constant storm in our lives. The disciples in the storm had every right to be afraid. They were fighting for their lives, and so are we.

Are you gripped with fear because of a storm currently taking place in your life? Are the difficulties of life causing anxiety around you and wearing you down? Perhaps you are dealing with a situation where you're not quite sure how you even ended up there and you have no idea of the outcome. Some of you have been in the storm for a while and have no idea how to get out of this; you have resigned yourself to the thought that this is how life will always be. Like some of the disciples in the boat, you are doing everything in your power just to stay afloat. I've been there.

Many of us lose sight of the fact that Jesus is with us during our rough times. Sure, He is with us during the good times; isn't that why we have good times? But how can Jesus be with us during the challenges we face in life? I tend to think that if Jesus is with me, if He is blessing me, if I were experiencing His favor, then I wouldn't have tough times. It should be smooth sailing, shouldn't it? My marriage would be great, my kids wouldn't talk back and I wouldn't have to deal with the aches and pains of getting older. But the truth is we come to a better understanding of God in our pain than in our triumphs. That is what this book will show you.

Throughout this book, we will walk through the event depicted in Rembrandt's painting by looking specifically at Matthew 8:23–27. One would be hard pressed to find a more action-packed passage of Scripture than the whole chapter of Matthew 8. We don't know the amount of time that passes during the chapter. It could have taken place over the course of several days or weeks, but we do know Jesus was busy and the results were impressive. From dealing with large crowds who were enthralled by His ability to heal both lepers and demoniacs, to being moved by the faith of a centurion; faith, fear and healing are all central themes. All this busyness leads to Jesus and His followers getting away on the Sea of Galilee so He can display his most impressive attribute—having command over Creation.

In chapter one, we will cover the sometimes crushing weight disappointment heaps upon our shoulders. We've all experienced the dreaded moment when someone, usually a parent, said, "I'm not angry with you. I'm just disappointed." What do we do when we feel God is disappointed in us? How do we begin to make amends for our own perceived actions and behavior we think has drawn God's disappointment?

God's Word tells us that He values obedience over sacrifice. In chapter two we'll discuss how can we put this discipline into practice, when it seems to go against our nature to obey.

Challenging life events are something we all go through. If God loves us as His Word says He does, then there must be purpose to our troubles. The question is, who do we turn to when times get tough? We'll dig into the topic of life's troubles in chapter three.

With fear being a universal emotion, we will learn in chapter four how we process fear differs from individual to individual. Who we turn to while being fearful demonstrates where our faith lies.

Chapter five is about desperation. The disciples were desperate to survive the storm and were forced to choose between two approaches—battling the storm themselves or going to Jesus for help.

In chapters six and seven we will cover two aspects of faith—how our experiences can take us to a crossroads to see what we really believe, and how faith is an action that requires stepping out. Faith is a key ingredient in our ability to overcome the fears of life. But exercising our faith is rarely easy. Just like a muscle that must be tested in order to grow stronger, faith is that part of our spiritual walk with God that must be tested in order to be developed and strengthened over time.

With worship forming such an important element of our faith, we will learn in chapter eight how worship can take many forms. Ultimately, however, worship always ends up focused on the person of Jesus Christ.

Although I don't wish challenges on anyone, I do hope your faith in Jesus will grow as you draw closer to Him. It undoubtedly will. And I hope you enjoy this read. Jesus, Rembrandt and I will be with you every step of the way. May your faith be strengthened while your fear diminishes. Enjoy!

CHAPTER 1

DO I DISAPPOINT GOD?

"But he said to me, 'My grace is sufficient for you, for my
power is made perfect in weakness.'"
—Corinthians 12:9

*H*ave you ever felt that you disappoint God? I
don't know about you, but I feel like God is
disappointed with me…a lot. Sometimes I feel like I can never
quite get things right, like there is one sin (or many) I just
can't overcome. Certain behaviors are persistent, like my lack
of patience. I wish I could be more patient with my spouse,
more patient with my children. And I oftentimes wonder if
God is happy with what I've made of my life.

If you're like me, you might feel like you need to work
harder to please God so as not to disappoint Him. You may be
thinking that the storms in your life are happening because

God is disappointed in you. I want to dispel these thoughts at the very beginning of this book and tell you that God isn't disappointed with you. *At all*. Not even a little bit.

Several years ago, Philip Yancey wrote the hugely popular book, *Disappointment with God*. If I'm honest, I am constantly disappointed with God...because He never does what I think He should do! Do you ever feel like that? I think I have things figured out. I know why I deserve that job, or that house or why I have this person as my spouse. So why doesn't God see what I see? At times, we all get disappointed with God, don't we? But the question I often ponder is, "Does God get disappointed with me?"

I recently posed a question to our church staff, "Do you ever feel that you disappoint God?" Some are people who have been Christians for just a few years, and some for over fifty years. A couple of them felt that they disappoint God because of bad teaching they experienced when they were younger. Pastors or teachers would try to scare the hell out of them, sort of scare them into Heaven. Maybe you have experienced that, also?

Others fear disappointing God because no matter the depths of their efforts, there is always the feeling of falling short of what they think God expects of them. One person talked about the influence of parents. This is big because we often project onto God the things that we experience with our parents whether good or bad. Because of this, some experts suggest that a parent should never say they are disappointed in their child because of the weight associated with that kind of statement. A child might feel, "Well, if my dad is disappointed in me, then God must be disappointed in me, too."

A couple other staff members said that God is disappointed in them because they don't keep up with the disciplines of Christian living—prayer, reading the Bible, going to church and so forth. A few of them also mentioned shame. I thought that was interesting because shame is powerful, isn't it? It's a close cousin of disappointment. If someone is disappointed in you, then you will probably also experience some degree of guilt and shame that goes along with it. Who wants any of that, right?

Whenever I dive into a topic, I always go to my favorite Bible study tool, blueletterbible.org. It is a great reference with dictionaries, commentaries and other extremely helpful resources. It has a nice feature where you can type in a word and it will tell you how many times that word appears throughout Scripture. For the heck of it, I typed in the word "disappoint" using the New International Version (NIV) translation. Guess how many times the word "disappoint" appears in Scripture? Zero! Zero results turned up. I thought that couldn't be right, so I tried the New American Standard translation with one result:[1]

"And hope *does not disappoint* because the love of God has been poured out within our hearts through the Holy Spirit who was given to us" (emphasis mine).

Hope does not disappoint.

The conclusion? Nowhere in Scripture does it say that God is ever disappointed in us. We must remind ourselves that God loves us more than we will ever know. You see, the Father heart of God is one that doesn't experience disappointment with us. The Father heart of God doesn't feel shame toward us. Can you take a moment and say this out loud?

I am not a disappointment to God.

Personally, I feel like this is such an important statement to make because it is a game changer. Many of us have gone our whole lives thinking we are failures, that we don't measure up —we are a disappointment to God. Some of us may not even be able to say the words, "I am not a disappointment to God," because we don't really believe it. Many of us have the idea in our head that God is this cosmic ogre who has His arms crossed, shaking His head in disgust when He thinks of us. I want you to know this is a lie. It is a skewed view of God, and Satan loves it when we don't have a clear view of who God is. God has nothing but love for you. It doesn't mean He isn't saddened by our poor choices, by our sins. He doesn't affirm everything we do. I have three kids. They do some of the craziest things. I don't affirm everything that they do. I am saddened when they do stupid things. When they start doing crazy things, I call them on it to correct them. Why? Because I love them. It's the same with God.

Another thing to remember is that God is easily pleased with you but is never satisfied. For those of us who have had children, think back to when your baby took his or her first steps. I remember with our first child, my wife and I spent what was probably hours rejoicing over Jack's first steps. We would sit on the ground and watch him walk back and forth between us. We were thrilled but we weren't satisfied. We knew that Jack would go on to greater things, like walking and running and riding a bike. You are thrilled when your child reaches each of those milestones, but you are not satisfied. It's the same with God. God is pleased with us when we are fulfilling His will. But He's not satisfied because He has greater things in store for us, including when we reach glory in Heaven.

Consider also that God isn't shocked by anything. God has seen it all. He is all-knowing. And because of this, He never says, "Man, I didn't see that one coming." He knows that although we are the peak of His creation, we are fallible, sinful creatures. He knows what we are made of, and despite that, He still pursues us.

There is no better example of God in pursuit in all of Scripture than in the life of Peter. On the last night of his life, Jesus gathered his closest friends for an intimate dinner.

Then Jesus told them, "This very night you will all fall away on account of me, for it is written:

'I will strike the shepherd,
and the sheep of the flock will be scattered.'

But after I have risen, I will go ahead of you to Galilee."

Peter replied, "Even if all fall away on account of you, I never will!"

Peter is feeling pretty good about himself. Pretty confident, wouldn't you agree? Jesus goes on to tell Peter what was going to happen next by saying:

"I tell you the truth this very night before a rooster crows, you will disown me three times." But Peter declared, "Even if I have to die with you, I will never disown you." And all the other disciples said the same.[2]

A short time later, Jesus' words came true.

Now Peter was sitting out in the courtyard, and a servant girl came to him. "You also were with Jesus of Galilee," she said.

But he denied it before them all. "I don't know what you're talking about," he said.

Then he went out to the gateway, where another girl saw him and said to the people there, "This fellow was with Jesus of Nazareth."

He denied it again, with an oath: "I don't know the man!"

After a little while, those standing there went up to Peter and said, "Surely you are one of them, for your accent gives you away."

Then he began to call down curses on himself and he swore to them, "I don't know the man!"

Immediately a rooster crowed. Then Peter remembered the word Jesus had spoken: "Before the rooster crows, you will disown me three times." And he went outside and wept bitterly.[3]

Of Jesus' twelve disciples, Peter was one of the "Big Three." Peter, James and John were the disciples who were closest to Jesus. Peter was big, he was bold, he was brash, borderline arrogant and confident in who he was as a person. Remember, Peter is the one who stepped out of the boat and walked on water towards Jesus. When Jesus told his disciples that He must go to Jerusalem and die, Peter in his boldness corrected Jesus and said, "Never Lord, this shall never happen to you." Peter is the one who, when the mob came to arrest Jesus, cut off the ear of the High Priest's servant. Peter is the one who told Jesus that even though everyone else would desert Him, he never would.

And now Peter was left alone, a tragic figure, weeping because he saw his failings as a person. He saw his failings as a friend, his failings as a follower of Jesus. He recognized that Jesus saw right through his blustery, confident persona and knew Peter better than he knew himself. What Peter was feeling was disappointment with himself. He not only let Jesus down, but embarrassingly and publicly, he let himself down. In short, Peter came face to face with his own inadequacy. I think our feelings of inadequacy oftentimes lead us to believe we are a disappointment to God.

Several years ago, Dos Equis beer ran a hugely successful marketing campaign where they introduced the "Most Interesting Man in the World." These are probably my all-time favorite commercials. If the "Most Interesting Man in the World" suffers from anything, feelings of inadequacy are not one of them. He can speak French in Russian. When he goes for a swim, dolphins appear. His blood smells like cologne. He doesn't cry when he dices onions, and he can walk a chihuahua and still look masculine. I mean, this is the guy who can do it all, right?

However, for Donny Abbott, and I suspect for many of us, it's a bit of a different story. This lie of believing that we disappoint God really stems from feeling inadequate. Feelings of inadequacy happen for several reasons.

1. *We compare ourselves to others.* I personally tend to feel inadequate as I look around and begin to think, "Why can't I do that?" or "Why can't I have that?" "Why can't I have more money, or be taller or better looking...," and on and on my thoughts go. And because I don't live up to what I'm comparing myself to, I begin to feel that God is disappointed with me.

2. *Being put down by influential people in our lives.* For many of us that usually goes back to our fathers. Perhaps you were someone who never quite lived up to your father's expectations for you. If you are married, interactions with your spouse can also lead to feelings of inadequacy.

3. *Falling short as a Christian.* When it comes to God

you might be thinking, "If God only knew the things I've done, He wouldn't want anything to do with me." Or perhaps you're trying this Christian thing, but you don't really like church, you can't find your way around a Bible, and therefore, you feel inadequate and God must be disappointed with you.

There are many more areas I could mention but what I want to remind us all is that God has created each of us for a purpose. And God has you exactly where He wants you, as imperfect as you are. As inadequate as you may feel, God has a plan for you. Our typical response to inadequacy and disappointment is to work harder,

...to go to church more,

...to read our Bible more,

...to volunteer more,

...to tithe more.

We engage in these practices and other things thinking they will help us feel better about ourselves and get us back into a right relationship with God so that He is not disappointed with us. The problem with this approach is that we fail, don't we? The other problem with this is that you and I can never do enough to get back into a right relationship with God on our own.

The truth is that feeling God is disappointed with us is really an identity issue. You and I have a choice every day to gauge our value and worth based on the thoughts, feelings, words and actions of others, or we can choose to believe what God says about us. So, what does God say about us?

Let me first remind you that God's Word is a story that depicts how much He loves you. In the story, God is the pursuer of man. And God goes to great lengths to find His lost children. Remember in the garden after Adam and Eve sinned, they went into hiding? God pursued them and asked them what I think is the most haunting question in all of Scripture, "Where are you?" Of course, God knew where they were physically. He asked that question of them so that they could see where they were in *their* relationship with God. "Where are you?" is a question asked by someone who is pursuing. God is constantly pursuing people.

He offers forgiveness for our waywardness; He performs miracles on our behalf; He's even given a piece of himself and sacrificed His Son. He does the types of things we would do to pursue our own wayward children. You and I would do anything to get our children back. And some of you have. So, in the story of God, what does that say about you? About me? Why would God go to such great lengths to win us back? It's because you and I have inherent value and worth to God. He pursues you because He desperately loves you. God isn't disappointed in you in the least. Brennan Manning writes in his book *The Ragamuffin Gospel:*

"He is not moody or capricious; He knows no seasons of change. He has a single relentless stance toward us: He loves us. He is the only God that man has ever heard of who loves sinners. False gods—the gods of human manufacturing—despise sinners, but the Father of Jesus loves all, no matter what they do. But of course, this is almost too incredible for us to accept.[4]"

That sounds too good to be true, doesn't it? It's hard to believe that God would pursue us because so many of us give up on one another too easily. But God doesn't give up on you. He's your number one fan. He wouldn't pursue you if He felt you weren't worth it or if He were disappointed in you. Our identity is not found in what others think of us, or what we can do, or how much money we have or any other external factor. Our value and worth and adequacy come in the simple fact that you and I are children of the Most High God. The apostle Paul reminds us:

"Not that we are competent in ourselves to claim anything for ourselves, but our competence comes from God.[5]"

What if I told you that any feelings of inadequacy you have might actually be a good thing? That your areas of weakness are places where God can truly shine in your life? Chuck Swindoll says:

"Inadequacy forces us to rely fully on God for power and strength. That's where He can do His best work—in your weakness…He doesn't use super-strong, self-assertive, self-centered people. He uses weak, trembling, inadequate, ill-equipped people—people just like you and me.[6]"

And as we read the Scriptures, they show us that God clearly does His best work through people He could have easily been disappointed in, people who were inadequate. The Scriptures tell story after story of people who were drunks or liars or womanizers or adulterers. People who you would never think could be used by God. But if you read your Bible, you know that God did some amazing things through these pretty ordinary, sinful people. I don't know about you, but that's good company to be in. God wasn't disappointed in them, and He's not disappointed in you.

Back to our friend Peter. After his denial of Jesus, Peter went back to fishing—the only thing he knew how to do. One morning after pulling an all-nighter and not catching anything, guess who shows up?

Jesus!

He shows up not to just cook Peter a breakfast, but instead to invite Peter back into a right relationship with him. To tell Peter *and* show Peter that He is not disappointed in him. And to remind him that Jesus has big plans for him.

When they had finished eating, Jesus said to Simon

Peter, "Simon son of John, do you truly love me more than these?"

"Yes, Lord," he said, "you know that I love you."

Jesus said, "Feed my lambs."

Again Jesus said, "Simon son of John, do you truly love me?"

He answered, "Yes, Lord, you know that I love you."

Jesus said, "Take care of my sheep."

The third time he said to him, "Simon son of John, do you love me?"

Peter was hurt because Jesus asked him the third time, "Do you love me?" He said, "Lord, you know all things; you know that I love you."

Jesus said, "Feed my sheep.[7]"

God in pursuit over breakfast. Asking a variant of the question that was asked of Adam in the garden. Jesus wanted to know the condition of Peter's heart and where he was in his relationship with God. It is interesting that after the resurrection Peter was one of the first people to whom Jesus revealed himself. We don't know what took place in their conversation, but we do know that in this situation, this meal at breakfast, Jesus wanted to publicly acknowledge Peter and extend grace and mercy to him.

It shouldn't be lost on any of us that three times Jesus asked Peter if he loved him. Why would He ask Peter three times if he loves Him? He did so as a way of redeeming the three times that Peter denied knowing Jesus. It was also important for Jesus to restore Peter in the presence of others because Peter had denied Jesus in the presence of others. It was important for Peter to hear that Jesus wasn't disappointed in him, but instead had great things planned for Peter. Jesus knew that Peter would be the one who the Church would be built upon. That doesn't sound like a disappointed God to me.

Why would Jesus do all of this?

Because God is a god of second chances.

The chance to redeem ourselves and to be redeemed by God always comes through the person of Jesus Christ. As I said earlier, you and I can never do enough to get back into a right relationship with God. We can't do enough so we have to rely on the grace of God instead. And grace is in short supply in our world, isn't it? *Man, you mess up today and you're going to pay for it.*

Grace is different in God's economy. God sees through our outward appearances and knows we are just like Peter, whose redemption will be discussed later in the book. We are simply frail human beings, desperately in need of His grace; getting what we don't deserve.

In 2000, the rock band, U2, recorded a song called *Grace*; it was the last song on their album. The song is about how God finds beauty and goodness in you despite your mistakes. Don't believe for a minute that any storm you are currently going through is because God is disappointed in you.

Questions for Discussion

1. Do you ever feel that you disappoint God?
2. How do you view God? As a cosmic ogre or a loving father?
3. How have you experienced feelings of inadequacy due to: a) Comparing yourself to others? b) Being put down by influential people in your life? c) Falling short in what think a Christian should be?

CHAPTER 2

OBEDIENCE

"Then he got into the boat and his disciples followed him."
—Matthew 8:23

The book of Matthew is a fascinating book meant to portray Jesus as the Messiah, the one to usher in the "Kingdom of Heaven." In chapter eight Matthew highlights His messianic attributes by way of supernatural abilities. It is a chapter where Jesus performs numerous healings, like curing lepers, those with fevers and delivering the demon possessed. As you read through these events, it seems like they all occurred one right after the other over the course of a day. We don't know if it all took place over the course of one day, several days, weeks or months.

What we do know is that after Jesus healed Peter's mother-in-law and numerous demon-possessed people, He and His followers got into a boat and headed out onto the Sea of Galilee. Was it a leisurely evening out on the lake due to Jesus having just finished teaching a large group of people? Perhaps He simply wanted to get away after an exhausting day. That wouldn't have been an unusual thing for Jesus to do. We know He would frequently go off by Himself to pray. So quite possibly, as Jesus and His followers are pushed to the lake's edge to avoid being overtaken by a large crowd, they got into the boat because they simply needed a break.

One of my favorite things to do is to venture out on a boat. There is nothing quite like the rocking of a boat and hearing the water gently lapping against the hull. Although I have never owned a boat, I have taken many excursions with friends who have them. A trip to Catalina, a day cruise to Ensenada, Mexico, many deep-sea fishing trips and even a week-long trip around the Caribbean; all of them were memorable experiences out on the water. Probably my favorite place to go boating is Lake Tahoe. As the largest alpine lake in North America, it is arguably one of the most picturesque. Lake Tahoe is surrounded by the beautiful Sierra Nevada Mountains and known for its amazing water clarity, water sports and fishing. Being out on this lake is truly a breathtaking experience.

For a sheer adrenaline rush, however, there is nothing quite like river rafting. Having experienced everything from Class II rapids on the Merced River, to Class V on the Kings River, rafting a scenic river is an experience you will never forget. The key to having a fun rafting trip where everyone in your raft survives is listening to and obeying the guide. Your rafting guide is usually someone who has several years of rafting experience and is in tune with the various nuances of the river. Understanding the river is critical in successfully navigating any hidden dangers that might be lurking below the surface. Avoiding potential pitfalls requires the participants to listen and heed the commands of the guide. In other words, the key behavior for a successful trip is *obedience*.

Now immediately when you hear the word "obedience" it conjures up different emotions, doesn't it? To obey someone implies you are subjecting yourself to do something they tell you to do. Admittedly, it requires a certain amount of humility to be obedient. That can be a good or bad thing. As a passenger in a raft, responding with obedience can literally mean the difference between life and death. Most people who raft willingly obey the orders of the guide. But what happens if you don't trust the person you are required to obey?

In March of 1974, a fifty-two-year-old man in green fatigues came out of hiding on the Philippine Island of Lubang. He looked to be in good health and even his rifle was in good working order. So, what's this guy's story?

There had been rumors and reported sightings of him for many years amongst people who lived in the surrounding villages. But it wasn't until his former commander, Major Yoshimi Taniguchi, was flown to where the soldier was hiding out, that the mystery man finally emerged from the jungle.

Major Taniguchi told Hiroo Onoda that it was okay, he could finally surrender. In 1944, Onoda was an Intelligence Officer in the Japanese Imperial Army. The last orders he received just prior to America's invasion of the island were from his commander, who said:

> "You are absolutely forbidden to die by your own hand. It may take three years, it may take five, but whatever happens, we'll come back for you. Until then, so long as you have one soldier, you are to continue to lead him. You may have to live on coconuts. If that's the case, live on coconuts! Under no circumstances are you [to] give up your life voluntarily."

On that March day when Onoda came out of hiding, he had the distinction of being one of the last Japanese soldiers to surrender from World War II.[1]

In a very real, practical way, Onoda lived out the act of obedience. Although he fought for values that were contrary to what America stood for, one must still admire his obedience. Onoda had a choice to make like we all do. We all have an opportunity to be obedient to the authority in our lives. And that's another thing obedience comes down to—the issue of *authority*. There are a lot of competing voices in our world, all attempting to tell us what to do or believe about a plethora of topics. So, the question for all of us to ponder is, "Who is in authority over my life today?"

Onoda knew who his authority was and lived out his obedience every single day. Surely, he had times of uncertainty; times where he doubted if it was worth what he was doing. In spite of any doubts or fears he experienced, he continued to obey even to the point of living on the island for twenty-nine years after the Japanese formally surrendered, signaling the end of the war! And here lies the crux of obedience—doing something you may not necessarily want to do because the one in authority over you told you to.

As we read through the Scriptures, it seems that what defines a person's walk with God is his or her willingness to be obedient to what God has called them to do even if they don't understand why. Consider the case of Abraham when God told him to leave everything and "go to the land I will show you.[2]" Another example is doing something even when it seems outrageous, like Noah did when he built the ark God told him to build.[3] And how about Jonah? God asked him to do something he flat out didn't want to do. He eventually came around and obeyed God.[4] Obedience matters to God. In fact, the prophet Samuel tells us it is what God desires most:

> But Samuel replied: "Does the LORD delight in burnt offerings and sacrifices as much as in obeying the LORD? To obey is better than sacrifice, and to heed is better than the fat of rams.[5]"

The Hebrew word for obedience is shama, which means

"to hear." People throughout the Bible would often hear a directive from the Lord that usually began with something like, "And the Lord said," or "So God said." Once God said it, though, His expectation was that people would hear the instruction and then do what was asked of them. They were to follow through in obedience under the authority of God. Jesus' brother solidifies this when he said, "Do not merely listen to the word, and so deceive yourselves. Do what it says.[6]"

Adam, Eve, Abraham, Noah, Jonah, Moses—all of these people were faced with a decision to obey or not after they had heard from God. They all had a real-life dilemma standing in front of them—one that was usually foreboding, intimidating and overwhelming. One where their own lives and the lives of others were at stake. You might think that if you receive a directive from God, then what's the problem, right?

One of the aspects I love about the Scriptures is that it shows the character flaws of all the people in it. An example of which is seeing how Moses wanted nothing to do with facing Pharaoh. He even told God to have his brother do all of the talking because he was embarrassed about his speech impediment. We read that it took two attempts to get Jonah to overcome his fear of the people of Ninevah. When God told Jonah to travel to Ninevah and tell the people there—who at that time were the most brutal force on Earth—to turn from their wicked ways, he didn't do it the first time God told him to, but he did eventually end up practicing obedience. And by doing so God used him to change the hearts and minds of countless numbers of people.

Many of our biblical heroes expressed fear and trepidation despite the assurance that God would be with them. They lived in the tension of whether they would follow that directive and be obedient or not. Even Jesus had a decision to make about dying on the cross. He cried out to God in anguish for another way to save mankind, and thankfully, He obeyed. It comes down to authority and trust. All of these people understood God as their ultimate authority, and they trusted Him.

Was obedience present in our story of Jesus and the disciples out on the lake? I think it was. But this obedience wasn't something they just blindly went about doing. To follow someone takes *trust*. Over the time they had spent with Jesus, they had learned to trust *and* obey Him. So, did Jesus *tell* them to get into the boat or was it more of an invitation? Getting into the boat with Jesus was something they had probably done dozens of times before. Their trust in Him was without question. One must wonder, however, if they would have been so obedient had Jesus told them while they were standing on the shore that they were heading into a deadly storm, one that would threaten their lives and try every ounce of their being.

Would they have gone had they known Jesus would be sleeping while they were going through this storm, making it seem like they were on their own, or that He didn't care they were going to die? Even if Jesus had told them that going through the storm would grow their faith if they put their trust in Him, how many would have stayed on shore? I wonder how many of them would have just said, "You know what, Jesus, I'm good. You guys go on without me." But none of them stayed behind. All of them followed Jesus in trust and obedience.

Jesus didn't tell His close friends what was awaiting them, just like He doesn't reveal the trials and tribulations that await us. Or even the outcome of those tribulations. What He does tell us is to be obedient to Him, to the calling that He has placed on our lives, especially in times of trouble.

What storm are you facing right now that you are unsure of the outcome? Perhaps it is that one child of yours who has always sort of done things his or her own way. And now, because of poor decisions, he or she is living in your basement with no job and seemingly no hope for the future. His or her friends, who you never cared for, are constantly at your house. You know this is a situation that isn't good. You want to help, and in the past, you have. But now your child is at an age when they need to accept some adult responsibility. As his parent, what do you do? How is God asking you to be obedient? Where do you need to trust Him?

Is there an area in your personal life where you haven't completely been obedient to God? Something is getting in your way—an addiction, insecurity, spending or maybe anger. What is keeping you from obeying? Are the stakes too high? Are you too prideful? Too embarrassed? Filled with regret? Is there another authority in your life other than God pulling at you? Maybe you have had a nagging feeling for some time now that God is asking you to take control of that thing controlling you. No matter what the outcome, you can trust God.

Or, perhaps you are at a crossroads in your work life. Maybe you've been in a stable job for twenty years and you feel God is calling you to move on to something else, but you're afraid to leave the steady income and consistency. And in the process, you are dying inside. Of course, God wants us to provide for our families but is He calling you into something grander? Something that will have more of an impact on the Kingdom? I know it's scary. It was for Peter. For Paul. For John. But today we remember their names not for their lack of obedience but because of it. So, go ahead and obey what God is calling you to do. Get in the boat and trust Him with the outcome. You'll be glad you did.

Questions for Discussion

1. In your situation, what risks do you face by being obedient to God?
2. What could the likely outcome be for your obedience? Your disobedience?

3. What have you been putting off that you know you need to follow through with to be obedient?

4. Why is being obedient so hard?

5. How are obedience, trust and authority interwoven?

CHAPTER 3

TROUBLE

"Suddenly a furious storm came up on the lake, so that the
waves swept over the boat..."
—Matthew 8:24

We all experience getting into trouble at some point in our lives, more often when we are young. The lesson's we learn when we are young help us to see there are consequences when we make poor decisions. And we all know decisions don't happen in a vacuum but can impact many people.

When my oldest son, Jack, was in third grade he thought it would be a good idea to grab some money that was lying on our kitchen counter. The five hundred dollars was the money my father-in-law had just paid me for rent earlier that morning. I didn't notice the money was missing until I received a phone call from the principal at my son's elementary school, calling to inform me that Jack was passing out twenty-dollar bills to his buddies. While this most definitely made Jack the most popular kid at school, it didn't exactly endear him to his parents. I made my way over to the school and, fortunately, was able to recover all the money. Jack, however, found himself in a lot of trouble.

Many times, trouble can be found in mischievous adventures, such as my son's experience. Most of the time, though, trouble is unsettling and can happen unexpectedly. It seems to come from nowhere and catches us when we least expect it. One day, we are seemingly secure in our lives and then everything changes in the blink of an eye. We're not sure how or why it happened. Nothing is as it was before.

The life storms we experience can be so overwhelming, so intense, they leave us powerless. Like the time when my friends and I were rafting one summer along the beautiful Merced River that flows through the Yosemite Valley in Central California. We had just come through a stretch of Class III rapids, when suddenly, our raft hit something hidden under the water. We came to an abrupt stop, and before I knew it, I found myself hurtling into the freezing cold water. Completely unprepared, I was heading towards a huge granite rock face while the river was making a sharp, hairpin turn to the left. I avoided the wall by pushing off from the rock face with my feet, and thankfully, within a few minutes, I was back in the raft armed with a great story to tell.

Suddenly being thrown from the raft scared me to death, and I'm so grateful I survived the incident with nothing more than a bruised ego! The most shocking thing about the whole situation was how quickly my rafting trip changed from a blissful adventure on a beautiful day to a perilous event that could have ended badly.

This kind of sudden trouble is where the disciples found themselves on the Sea of Galilee that day. The Sea of Galilee is a freshwater lake located in the Jordan Rift Valley. On its northwestern shore sits Kibbutz Ginosar, a small, sleepy, present-day Israeli village of less than six hundred people. Jesus-followers are more familiar with its biblical name, Gennesaret.

A curious find occurred there in 1986. At that time, the sea had receded several meters due to a drought that had lasted many years. In the winter of that year, two local fisherman, brothers Moshe and Yuval Lufan, were out walking along the shoreline and noticed, not far from shore, an odd-shaped object protruding from the mud. Upon closer inspection, they discovered that this object was, in fact, a *very* old fishing boat. Soon word got out, and the excitement of their discovery spread throughout the village and the surrounding region.

Over the next twelve days, hundreds of locals and scholarly archaeologists descended upon their location. What these brothers discovered, by chance, was a vessel that had been buried in mud for over two thousand years. Carbon dating revealed that this boat dated back to the first century.

The boat has since become known as the "Jesus Boat" or the "Sea of Galilee Boat." This boat, although showing her age, was in excellent shape, having been preserved in the mud for over two millennia. It's fair to say that the boat Jesus and his followers rode in was very similar to this one. The "Jesus Boat" measures roughly twenty-seven feet long and is about seven and one-half feet wide, and now sits in the Beit Yigal Allon Museum, where thousands of people visit it every year.

To call this discovery amazing is an understatement. Seeing something that is two thousand years old naturally brings forth lots of questions. Who built it? Who rode in it? How many years did this boat sail around the Sea of Galilee? Is it possible that Jesus and His followers travelled on this very boat? Considering the Matthew passage, why did they need to go to the other side of the lake in the first place? Lucky for us, we can find the answer to this question in the Scriptures.

Matthew tells us they were looking to get away from the crowds to rest, and the only place they could go was out on the lake. What the disciples didn't know was they were headed right into a life-changing storm. Soon after they moved away from shore, a storm (or squall) came down upon the lake.

The Sea of Galilee sits at 680 feet below sea level, making it the lowest freshwater lake in the world. Squalls like the one described in Matthew 8 happen frequently there, because right above the lake, warm and cool air converge due to the two-thousand-foot-tall hills to the east that hold in the onshore air flow blown in from the Mediterranean Sea to the west. This atmospheric gathering creates sudden and violent storms that can come on quickly at any time. A boat and its crew caught in one of these fierce storms faces certain trouble.

When we read the word *squall,* we immediately get the idea that it involves wind and rain, and it's probably not good. In the New American Standard translation, the storm is described as a "fierce gale.[1]" A gale, by definition, is a sustained wind anywhere from thirty-two to seventy-two miles per hour. Anything above that and the storm is classified as a hurricane. Whatever it was, squall or gale, the Sea of Galilee was well known for generating such storms. This storm was so vicious that the disciples surely believed they were facing certain death.

Keep in mind that several of the disciples were long-time fishermen; they knew the sea well and had been through their share of storms. However, something was different about this one. They knew they were in trouble, and fear was kicking in. Scripture reveals this by describing the way they cried out, "Lord save us, we are going to drown!" The waves were crashing around them, water was pouring in and thunder and lightning were crashing and flashing. These guys were in for it, and they realized they didn't have much time left to stay afloat.

Rembrandt's take on this scene depicts the different ways that those in the boat reacted to their trouble. And the way they reacted is probably similar to how you have reacted at different times when trouble has come your way. The guys at the top half of the boat are fighting the storm with all their might. The guy on the rudder is trying to change course, hoping that his efforts will guide them to safety. There is one sailor who looks to be grabbing Jesus in anger as if he is saying, "Why did You allow this to happen; don't You see what is going on?" There is even one guy who is just frozen in fear, unsure of which way to go or what to do. Perhaps he is thinking that if he does anything, it will only make the situation worse. So, the only thing he does is...nothing. And then finally there is the man who seemingly is resigned to his fate, and in his time of need, he turns to the one person he knew could help them. And to his dismay, He was asleep, or so it seemed.

Of the many threads that weave their way throughout Scripture, suffering and trouble are two of the most common. Perhaps this is because they are shared amongst people everywhere. At some point all of us encounter trouble or suffering. This of course begs the question, why is there trouble and suffering in life to begin with? Without oversimplifying, suffering and troubles are the continued evidence of sin in our world. Beginning with the fall of man in the garden of Eden, all of Creation suffers the penalty of Adam's sin.[2] The results of this are our poor choices that lead to trouble, or undue suffering caused by the sinful decisions of others. Whatever it is, and whoever is responsible for it, we all suffer or will suffer in our lifetime.

If the sufferings of man are inevitable and common to all, surely there must be some purpose to our troubles. Our finite minds and limited understanding of the way God works can't fathom it. So, one thing we all try to do is avoid trouble and suffering as much as possible, not realizing what God has for us in it. Noted author C. S. Lewis says:

"We can ignore even pleasure. But pain insists upon being attended to. God whispers to us in our pleasures, speaks in our conscience, but shouts in our pains: it is his megaphone to rouse a deaf world.[3]"

Suffering draws us closer to God. It wakes us up! Nothing takes us out of the normal rhythms of life as does pain and suffering. Jesus' brother, James, gave us some additional insight into the purpose of life's troubles by adding:

"Consider it pure joy, my brothers and sisters, whenever you face trials of many kinds, because you know that the testing of your faith produces perseverance. Let perseverance finish its work so that you may be mature and complete, not lacking anything.[4]"

According to James, then, another purpose of our troubles and trials is to develop character and perseverance, so we can mature in our faith. For some reason, trouble tends to be a stronger purifier to our faith than when times are going well.

So, if we know that trouble and suffering are faith builders, then how we respond when difficulties arise should be a clear indicator of the strength of our faith. I frequently wonder why it must be this way. I don't know if you're like me, but when tough times come my way, I tend to think I must have done something to deserve it. This brings up another idea that many people express—when we experience God's favor and blessing, He must be happy with us, versus when we experience trials in life, He must be unhappy with us. However, Jesus assures us that is not the case and provides us an example from the book of John where we read about a man blind from birth:

> "As He went along, He saw a man blind from birth. His disciples asked him, "Rabbi, who sinned, this man or his parents, that he was born blind?"
>
> "Neither this man nor his parents sinned," said Jesus, "but this happened so that the works of God might be displayed in him.[5]"

There is a pervasive view that those of great wealth are blessed, while the poor and people with disease and infirmities are cursed or have sinned. This view is as common today as it was in the day of Jesus.

The idea that we experience the trials and triumphs of life because God is unhappy with us couldn't be further from the truth. As we learned from the passage in John, the truth is that pain, suffering and trials of all kinds focus our attention and dependency on God. They build our character, increase our ability to persevere and equip us to minister to others who are going through similarly difficult life circumstances.

We also know that obedience versus disobedience isn't necessarily the reason or cause of suffering. It certainly can be if a person is engaging in activities they know they shouldn't be engaging in. But remember the disciples didn't do anything wrong—they were just following Jesus' instructions to get into the boat. An interesting take on this is offered by Bible commentator, Warren Wiersbe, who says:

> "Jonah ended up in a storm because of his disobedience, but the disciples got into a storm because of their obedience to the Lord.[6]"

The disciples obediently followed Jesus and still found themselves fighting for their lives. Why, do you think, would Jesus allow them to suffer in this way? If we think about it in the context of the James passage, Jesus must have thought they needed to mature in their faith. After all, it was only in the storm that Jesus could help His friends experience the miraculous themselves. Up until then they had witnessed Jesus perform miracles for others, but this time it was personal. Dary Northup, Senior Pastor of Timberline Church, says:

"You can be in the perfect will of God and be confused and disturbed. Don't let that annoy you. Know that God still has a plan."

These are reassuring words, aren't they? So how can we respond to the storms of life when they come upon us? When we are experiencing trouble in our lives, it can seem as if Jesus doesn't have a plan or a purpose. But just like He demonstrated to the disciples, He did have a plan and a purpose; in fact, He already knew the outcome! He knew they were going to make it to their destination, but first He wanted to develop their faith by way of a storm. He wants that for us sometimes too, and He uses trials and trouble to do so.

Like the paintings hanging in the Gardner Museum, our lives are not immune to trouble. With over a billion dollars' worth of art and rare artifacts, one might think that the Gardner was an impenetrable museum, with state-of-the-art security in place and a well-trained security staff. The truth is, however, that in 1990, due to budget constraints, the museum simply couldn't afford to put in the proper security precautions needed to protect the artifacts it stored. During the time leading up to the Gardner theft, in the late 1980s, criminals had hit most of the major art museums on the East Coast. Poor security and easy money to be made from stolen art left the Gardner vulnerable to a major heist.

Like the paintings, perhaps you feel your life is protected from trouble because of precautions you take or good and righteous things you do. You make good choices. Your life is going so well. You are a consistent churchgoer. You volunteer at your kids' school or for their sports team. You give to various charities, and you feel as if life is pretty good. That is until a storm hits.

How will you react? Will you be caught completely off-guard? Will you wonder how this could have happened and why? Will confusion set in, and will you begin asking God questions, like "Why is this happening?" and "Where are You, God?" Or, will you make pronouncements like, "If You really existed, this would not have happened!" and "God must not be a very good God if He is willing to let me suffer." Will the chaos of your trouble become too much, and will you begin questioning everything, even your faith?

These were the types of thoughts and questions my wife felt recently when a person she worked closely with over the last five years killed himself. She had no clue he would do such a thing and was caught off-guard by the suddenness of this event. She and countless others were left wondering if there were something that could have been done to change what happened. He left a storm behind, for sure, for his family and friends.

My wife and I have spoken several times about trying to make sense of this whole situation. I once asked her how his suicide affected her relationship with God. I wanted to know if she was angry at God for seemingly allowing this to happen. She said that she was never angry with God, but through this tragedy she had come to a better understanding of the presence of God and the finality of death. Her own thoughtfulness regarding the fragility of life has given her a deeper appreciation of people. Also, in the midst of such unimaginable grief, she has been reminded of this excerpt from a short devotion by Arthur Jackson that reads:

> "It's tempting to rationalize that the presence of trouble means the absence of God. But the truth of Scripture counters such notions. 'The LORD Almighty is with us; the God of Jacob is our fortress.[7] He is present when our circumstances are unbearable, and we find comfort in His character: He is good, loving, and trustworthy.[8]"

This is a great reminder as we face our fears in life.

Questions for Discussion

1. Share a time when sudden trouble came into your life.
2. What is your first response when faced with a troubling situation?
3. How has facing troubles in your past developed your character for the future?
4. How have troubles built or strengthened your faith?

CHAPTER 4

FEAR

"...but Jesus was sleeping."
—Matthew 8:24

*L*ooking at Rembrandt's painting, I am always drawn to certain aspects of the scene, such as the obvious chaos of men fighting the storm, Rembrandt looking out at me while holding his hat and the rope (yes, Rembrandt included himself in the painting), the guy struggling at the rudder and I always go to the guy at the top right of the boat. He is hard to miss as he is exhibiting what it means to literally be paralyzed by fear. His hands are close to his chest and he appears to be slightly backing away from the turmoil around him. His facial expression shows us he is clearly over his head and filled with fear.

The rest of his buddies are either frantically fighting the

storm or talking to Jesus. But he is doing the worst thing that can happen when troubles come our way—he's not doing anything except cowering in fear. He's not helping his buddies fight the storm at the top end of the boat, nor is he petitioning Jesus for help like the guys on the bottom half of the boat. He's doing absolutely nothing. Have you ever been at a place where you were paralyzed by your fears? A place where you literally didn't know what to do, and because of that, you did nothing?

That happened to me when my youngest was born. By all indications this was going to be a seemingly normal birth much like our previous two children. It was a wonderful spring day in Houston. A longtime, dear friend of ours was visiting from Washington, and we all settled into what we expected to be another witness to the incredible gift of life. But soon after the doctor entered the hospital room and broke my wife's water, all hell broke loose. Immediately, the baby started coming out, along with the umbilical cord on top of his head. I suspected this wasn't a good thing, as the doctor said, "We've got cord," and within seconds was on top of my wife with her hand holding the baby in place and a dozen other medical people quickly filled the room. Barking out orders, they prepared my wife for an emergency C-section; within seconds, they whisked her out the door leaving me, like the guy in the painting, cowering in fear.

The most perplexing figure in the Storm-on-the-Sea story isn't the cowering disciple, but Jesus himself. I can't imagine what the disciples must have felt like when, in their struggle, they noticed Jesus didn't seem to be bothered by the storm or the effects it was having on them. Something to remember is that four of the twelve disciples were fishermen. They were no strangers to storms on the sea. From the way they were reacting I'd say they believed the boat was going down and they were going to drown. I would venture to say their fear-level was high as they faced this storm. They didn't know if they were going to get through it or not.

This is an obvious problem with fear—you are just not sure what is going to happen next. You are not sure if God is there, and if He is going to do anything about your current situation. In fact, many times it can seem as if God is sleeping.

For years I have battled insomnia. Waking up at 2:30, 3:15, or 4:00 in the morning is a very common occurrence for me. While it does allow me to get in an early morning workout, it can be tough staying awake in the afternoon. Although waking early has been a problem for me, falling asleep is something that comes easily. However, one thing that I know I couldn't do is what Jesus did; sleep during a life-threatening storm. It is interesting to point out that this is the only passage in the New Testament that mentions Jesus doing the most basic of human things; sleeping. Perhaps He was displaying yet another supernatural ability by literally sleeping through *any* conditions.

There are a few things that come to mind when I read about Jesus sleeping. The first is how in the world could He possibly sleep during a storm in the middle of a lake? And secondly, why didn't He get up and help his partners out? You know "batten-down-the-hatches" kind of helping. Instead, it seems like His friends are left to fend for themselves, and with God in the boat, it *appeared* the disciples were left to face the storm and their fears alone.

At times, it can seem like we are alone when tough times come our way. When I'm facing a struggle, I think, "God, where are You? Are You sleeping? Do You see what I am going through right now?" It can seem as if we are left to battle our fears without the One who can overcome them. There is nothing more disheartening in life than feeling as if you are facing the storms of life alone. And this is the crux of the matter, isn't it?

When faced with loss of hope or experiencing feelings of despair, we know God could help us if He wanted to. So why doesn't He? Perhaps it's to remind us that God doesn't need us, but instead He wants us to have an awareness of our need for Him. So often we live our lives in a mode of self-sufficiency, and perhaps the storms of life are meant to remind us of our total dependency on God. It's interesting watching the progression of the disciples going from self-sufficiency in fighting the storm, to a point of desperation in reaching out to Jesus. Initially there was a sense of hope they could navigate the storm on their own until they reached a point of hopelessness and finally turned to Christ for help. That seems to be the order of progression we all take when we come up against a storm. We try to wage war with our fears by ourselves until we realize that some fears can only be faced with God by our side.

The word "fear" is a common theme throughout Scripture, appearing 271 times. There are several instances where people are told to "fear not." Several notable characters in Scripture are also reminded to "fear not for I am with you!" What a helpful reminder to them and for us that God is with us in the face of adversity. Author and psychologist, Dr. Chris Wilgers, says:

"Fear is an all-pervasive problem of humankind, and it cohabitates with us with great tenacity.[1]"

Hardwired into all human brains, fear is primarily a means of self-preservation. To maintain safety in our own lives and the lives of our loved ones, we will do whatever it takes to avoid being harmed, or worse. There are many things that we should have a healthy fear of, like snakes, fire, guns, the dark, heights. The list can go on and on. All these things have the capacity to hurt us if we don't treat them with proper respect.

Another aspect of fear is that it always involves loss. Pastor Gino Geraci at Calvary South Denver in Littleton, Colorado, spoke on this a few years ago in a sermon, stating how we are all fearful of losing essentially all the things in life that provide us with security, like our health, our jobs, our family or our futures. The oldest and strongest emotion in mankind is fear and the strongest fear is fear of the unknown.[2] My counseling friend, Dr. Renee Woodall, says that what adds to the unknown is a lack of control in our circumstances. So, as a way of combating our fear of loss, the unknown and lack of control, she says that we should think through "what are things that I can control?"

In our passage, we see the disciples trying to take control in what is an otherwise out-of-control situation. They are praying, taking down sails, holding the rudder, doing all they humanly can to survive. They were trying to avoid loss and seeking to take control of their situation. They inherently knew they couldn't control the weather, but they faced losing control of the boat in the storm. As the storm progressed and intensified, I wonder if they were also losing control of themselves. During this chaotic scene, the one person they knew could do something about both the external storm raging around them, and the internal one inside of each of them, wasn't doing anything.

Of course, the big thing with fear is that there are some things we cannot control. So, when things get out of control in your life, Dr. Woodall has a few suggestions you can follow:

1. Recognize your place of fear. Identify what is causing you to be fearful and see if there are triggers for the fear you can quite possibly avoid.
2. Ask what can I do? What do I have control of?

What actions can I take in the circumstances I am facing?

3. Give the situation you are facing to God by praying and giving your fear up to Him. Talk openly with Him about it. Tell Him how you are feeling; that you are scared and uncertain of the future.

4. Choose to have God's peace. Ask Him for it, and make daily, or sometimes minute-by-minute, decisions to walk in that peace.

Fear can also attack our identity, making us feel fearful and powerless as human beings. Is it possible that the fears in our lives really come down to where our identity lies? If you and I don't believe the things God says about us, if we forget where our identity lies, we will live defeated lives and not live out our identity in Christ.

This has been a struggle throughout most of my adult life. I have let fear steal my identity as a child of God. The interesting thing in my dealing with fear is that I'm usually a pretty fearless person when it comes to things of this world. I wouldn't say I'm an adrenaline junkie, but I've jumped out of airplanes, ridden motorcycles, gone river rafting and traveled to dangerous parts of the world. But when it comes to things not of this world, my fear really kicks in.

My fear has always been misguided, as it's never been of God or His angels. Instead, I have always been more fearful of Satan and his demons. Consequently, what has happened is that Satan has become the focus of my attention instead of God. This misguided fear started when I was twelve years old after watching the movie *The Exorcist*. That movie truly scarred me in ways I am only now fully realizing. Over the years, I have allowed that movie to affect my self-confidence and disrupt basic, normal adult behaviors.

As an example, there was a short period of time in my twenties when I was living alone that I became so afraid of taking a shower I began to take showers outside of the shower. It was as if I was doing the hokey pokey, putting one arm in, pulling one arm out. The reason for this craziness is that I was afraid the girl from *The Exorcist* was going to pop up over the shower curtain. For years, I had difficulty going to sleep with the lights off. In my fear, I experienced a loss of security and forgot that I am a child of God. I had forgotten that God is bigger than any fear that I have, or any demonic thing for that matter.

To overcome my fears and grow more confident in my walk with Christ, I had to identify myself with Christ and allow Him to help me. I had to change my thinking about who I am—about whose I am. I belong to Christ alone. It was during that time I decided to find a life verse, something that could give meaning to my relationship with God and help guide my life. I ended up with Romans 12:2a:

"Do not conform to the pattern of this world, but be transformed by the renewing of your mind."

This verse reminded me that I had to renew my thinking and align myself with the fact that I am a child of God. Memorizing this verse was an action step I could take to combat my fears. And as God's beloved child, I am reminded that He is in the boat with me, helping me to face my fears.

Susan, a friend of mine, has come to understand this truth in ways she never thought possible. In December 2017, her husband fell and hit his head on the concrete floor. She still isn't sure what may have caused his fall, but he ended up suffering a Traumatic Brain Injury (TBI) and will always be reliant upon her and others for his care. Her and her family's lives completely changed that fateful day. Over the course of the past couple of years, I have followed her husband's journey from afar and have read her CaringBridge journal entries.

Through her journal updates, she has captured the highs and lows of what it's like to care for someone with this type of an injury. Over a year later she is just now coming to terms with facing the rest of her life without the husband she once knew. Despite the difficulties of the past year and her fears of the unknown future, in one entry she wrote:

"God is greater. He gives us the power to live courageously, boldly, fearlessly in this life, when many things that surround us would tell us to be afraid. His truth whispers strong and sure to the deepest core of our spirits.[3]"

Susan is not allowing the enemy to use fear to shape her identity. She understands who she is and who is greater than any fear she will ever face.

Sometimes it takes God leading us to the depths of despair to truly understand the depth of His love. Lately I have been moved by the lyrics from the song "Oh My Soul" by Casting Crowns. If you get a chance to look them up, it would be worthwhile. This song captures the tension of facing our fears while trying to understand the truth that God is with us.

The lyrics of this song have incredibly deep meaning to the songwriter, John Mark Hall, the founder of the band. It came out of a time when Mark was facing a cancer diagnosis and was experiencing feelings of loss, hopelessness and the testing of his faith. He has shared in past interviews the internal conversation he was having with himself during the time of his diagnosis. As he faced the unknown, his feelings of fear kept slamming against something solid inside of him, which was his faith—his fears had to face the God he knew. He said that ultimately, he came to the realization that God had him and was in control. That was how I felt in that Houston hospital room, waiting to hear news that my wife and my son were ok. This was a situation that was completely out of my control. God was working through the hands of doctors and nurses to save the life of our baby. Thankfully after a cesarean delivery and spending a few days in the NICU, Wyatt did come home and has been a thriving kid ever since.

Like my experience in the shower and the experiences of

my friend Susan, the disciples and Mark Hall, we all came to a crossroads in our faith, and so will you. The fears we experience must face the God we know. We'll learn more about this in chapter five. When facing our fears, don't we all have to eventually ask the questions, "How big is my God? Is He bigger than my fears?" These were the kinds of questions the disciples faced, and in their time of testing and desperation, they reached out to God.

Questions for Discussion

1. What causes the most fear in your life? Why?
2. Has fear ever kept you from doing something you know you should do?
3. How has fear helped you grow your faith in Jesus?
4. Has your fear ever come up against the God you know? How big is your God?

CHAPTER 5

DESPERATION

"And they came to Him and woke Him, saying, 'Save *us*,
Lord; we are perishing!'"
—Matthew 8:25 (NASB)

A famous saying over the years, derived from the work
of Hippocrates, says, "Desperate times call for
desperate measures," which perfectly describes the situation I
was facing one fall day. I can still remember the feeling of
absolute panic that overcame me. I had just exited the C-130
aircraft and was having a seemingly good jump; parachute
opened, clear sky, little to no wind. And then about five
hundred feet off the ground, I saw nothing but green silk
around me.

This sky-high drama was playing out above the Sicily
Drop Zone in Fort Bragg, North Carolina. At the time, I was in

an Airborne unit—the 37th Engineer Battalion, and on this training jump, a fellow jumper had unwittingly "slipped" underneath me as we were descending to the ground. In the blink of an eye, this jump went from calm to chaos, and I was literally crawling on top of his parachute.

The ground was fast approaching and I was desperately clawing at the green silk of his parachute to get myself into the clear. I must confess that I wasn't very good at jumping out of airplanes. In many respects, it's an easy task—just hurl yourself out of the aircraft and wait for your chute to open. But there are many things that can go wrong, and when they do, a jumper has, as the Black Hat instructors at Jump School used to say, "You have the rest of your life to figure it out."

I only had nine jumps to my credit and three of the those were just awful experiences. This one just might have been the worst. In the end, I safely made my way off the parachute and had a successful landing. One very sobering aspect in the world of jumping out of airplanes is that any sort of equipment malfunction or mid-air accident leads a person to desperately try to save his own life.

Desperation is clearly evident in Rembrandt's painting. We see two ways of handling desperation that is so common to all of us. On the one hand, you have the five people at the top of the boat doing everything they possibly can to fight the storm and avoid drowning. At the bottom half of the boat, three of the occupants look to be having an animated conversation with Jesus. The disciples had tried everything humanly possible to save their own lives until they finally came to the realization that the situation was beyond what they could do. They absolutely needed divine intervention if they were to survive this tempest. So, in desperation, the disciples went to Jesus and woke Him, saying, "Lord, save us! We're going to drown!"

One has to chuckle at the irony of the scene. As the disciples were waging battle against the wind and the waves, the Creator of the wind and waves is right there in the boat with them taking a nap. In a last-ditch effort, they finally go to Christ to ask for His help.

Isn't that kind of how it is many times in our most dire of circumstances; we go to God only when we have exhausted all other avenues? I readily admit this is a common practice in my life so I'm not finding fault in any of us. We should all do everything we can to help ourselves in difficult situations. But it seems that we, or rather, *I* reach out to God only as a last resort.

To their credit, the disciples knew where to go in their time of need. In this impossible situation, they cried out to the God of the possible. We see this kind of scenario played out numerous times throughout Scripture—desperate people absolutely needing God to show up.

For twelve years, the woman had tried everything to cure her incessant bleeding. Without money or hope, she followed the crowd to see Jesus. Surely, she had heard about His ability to heal and had gone out of her way to see for herself if the rumors were true. And in the bustling of the crowd, she reached out to Him. For some reason, this woman in need is often depicted in paintings as being on the ground and reaching out in desperation to touch Jesus. Perhaps she is portrayed that way for dramatic effect. But the point is that in her desperation, she is vulnerable and eager to try anything to escape her current situation. She is throwing caution to the wind, and realizes she has nothing to lose.

Local doctors couldn't help the woman, and she was at a point of desperation in her life where she had nothing to lose and her health and well-being to gain. She could have frantically placed herself before Him face-to-face, grabbing His shoulders and begging for healing. But perhaps, understanding the cultural norms at the time, that would have been too much; instead, she took a subtler approach by touching the fringe of His cloak, not wanting to make a scene of this very personal situation. Matthew records:

> "She said to herself, 'If only I touch His cloak, I will be healed.[1]'"

Perhaps this was like the prayer many of us have prayed over the years. You know, "God would you give me just a little something —a sign to let me know that You are there, that You are watching out for me."

In fact, a co-worker found her husband this way. They had met through an online dating service, and prior to her first date, she asked God for a sign if this guy might be the one. When she was a little girl, her father used to call her "doll" as a term of endearment. So, my friend asked God for that word to be the sign that this man she was about to meet was the man she was supposed to marry.

After having a good time together, they hopped on his Harley and were about to head home when he turned to her and asked, "Okay, doll, are you ready?" She couldn't believe it. A couple of weeks and several more dates later, they talked about that moment. The guy said, "You know it is so weird as I have never used that term when talking to a woman before!" They ended up getting married a couple of months later.

I understand that probably most of the signs we ask God for don't happen. But the times when they do can confirm our belief that God is there. The morning the bleeding woman woke up, her prayer, her sign, was to be healed by Jesus' cloak. In desperation, on this day, she knew *something* had to change. She just couldn't continue unless God made a way. Apparently, it was the gravity of her situation and the faith in her heart that caused Jesus to stop everything and ask those closest to Him who had touched Him. Wherever Jesus went He drew crowds of people. People were probably always reaching out for Him, touching Him, and this scene was no different.

With a throng of people around Him, it was impossible to know who touched Him. But Jesus recognized something different about her touch; there was desperation in her need that caused Him to take notice. Healing power had gone out from Him and I imagine as Jesus stopped, almost in slow motion, He began looking at the dozens of faces surrounding Him, looking for the one who had touched Him. And finally, His eyes met hers.

"Then the woman, seeing that she could not go unnoticed, came trembling and fell at his feet. In the presence of all the people, she told why she had touched him and how she had been instantly healed. Then he said to her, "Daughter, your faith has healed you. Go in peace.[2]"

As the woman had discovered, there is something to humbling ourselves and admitting our need for God that draws His attention. We also see that with the tax collector, Zacchaeus, who, in desperation, climbed a tree to get a better look at Jesus. Upon seeing the great lengths Zacchaeus was willing to go to have a better view, Jesus invited Himself to Zacchaeus' home for dinner. When you're desperate for Jesus, you'll do whatever it takes to reach out to Him, including climbing a tree at the risk of being ridiculed by others. But ultimately, the acts of the bleeding woman and Zacchaeus changed their lives, and perhaps the lives of many others who were witnesses to the healing of the woman and the humility of a tax collector.

Most people, however, let pride and fear get in the way of reaching out to God for help. They haven't quite reached a point of desperation and still believe they are in control. These people don't want to admit their need for anyone, let alone for God. I have known many people over the years who were addicted to different substances to the point that it was causing problems, not just in their own life, but the lives of their loved ones. Despite this, they continued to live in denial about their problem. Either they were reluctant to admit they had a problem, or they were too prideful to reach out for help.

When the disciples cried out to Jesus, "Save *us*, Lord; we are perishing!" truer words have never been spoken. These were words that pertained to not just that moment but for all time. The disciples not only needed to be saved from the storm, but also from their sins. We all do. All of us need a Savior. The question is, do you recognize your need for a Savior, or not?

It usually takes some sort of major incident to cause a person to reach bottom and become desperate for change. This can range from your pants no longer fitting to your spouse threatening to leave or spending a night in jail because you had too much to drink. Everyone's moment of change is different. Ultimately, this moment is the point of desperation. You know, and everyone around you knows, something *must* change. Pastor Kyle Idleman asked a very insightful question in a sermon on desperate prayer, "When will your level of desperation override your pride?[3]"

For the bleeding woman, she was at the point where she didn't have any pride left. She was beyond that. Because of religious customs of the day, any remaining pride she had was stripped away. And with her incessant bleeding, she was religiously unclean. Being unclean greatly limited her interactions with the rest of the community. She was unable to go to the Temple, the one place where she could go and worship God like everyone else. Was there any sympathy amongst her family? Her neighbors? God? Did anyone take the time to see the world through her eyes as an outcast, one who was desperate for love and affection? Was there anyone who would pursue her in her condition and love her where she was? As a God of the marginalized, Jesus took notice and healed her. That day, Jesus took what was a humanly impossible situation and showed Himself to be the God of the possible.

I don't pretend to understand why God heals some people and doesn't heal others. Our job is to be faithful and pray diligently for healing. But if healing doesn't come about, and there is a resignation that things are not going to change, where does this leave a person? Some become bitter and give up altogether, while others exercise faith and believe that God has a plan—they have hope.

What we can learn from this event on the Sea of Galilee is that God is a God who can turn any situation around, no matter how dire the circumstances. That is the hope we all cling to, isn't it? That no matter how ominous the situation we face, after all other options have played themselves out, we still desperately turn to the One who can redeem what is nonredeemable, save what is un-savable, heal what is un-healable. And that's the point of the whole Gospel message—to provide hope and save that which is lost.

Hope is exactly what desperate people need. Desperate people want to change the situation they are in and will do so by any means necessary. If you are desperate, you will do whatever it takes to save your life or the life of others. The disciples in the boat with Jesus were both fighting the wind and waves and pleading with Jesus. It doesn't have to be one or the other. You can and should do whatever is humanly possible to get yourself out of the situation you are in, while also pleading to God for help.

What desperate circumstances are you facing? A drug addicted child? A financial situation with no end in sight? Are you going through a divorce and you feel like not only has your spouse abandoned you, but so has God? It's okay to be desperate. Maybe that is exactly the place where God wants you to be. A place where you are looking to Him. It might appear, in the situation with the disciples in the boat, that Jesus was indifferent to what His friends were going through. After all He *was* sleeping. It can seem the same with us also; that God doesn't care what is happening to us during difficult, challenging life events. But as the disciples learned, God did care and was there during the storm. During their darkest hour, when they needed Him most, He was there. And as a way of proving a point, Jesus awoke, stood up and rebuked the storm, and then turned to His followers and asked them, "Where is your faith?"

Questions for Discussion

1. Share a time where you were desperate for change and needed God to show up.
2. Desperation can be either reaching for something or clinging to something. Which situation do you most often find yourself in?
3. How has pride kept you from a more intimate relationship with God?

CHAPTER 6

THE CROSSROADS OF FAITH

"He replied, 'You of little faith, why are you so afraid?'"
—Matthew 8:26a

*a*nd just like that, with Jesus' words, the disciples were at a crossroads—one that would force them to discover the extent of their beliefs. The storm had finally subsided and the men's faces dripped with water. Their eyes squinted as they adjusted to the clearing of the clouds, the bright moon coming out from behind them. Everything was sopping wet. And Jesus wants to talk about faith...

Through heaving chests and panting mouths, it would have been easy for the disciples to quietly ask, "Why now? Why *this* time to talk about faith? You almost got us killed!" This might have been the time to ask Him why He wasn't pulling his weight during the storm. I can almost see them admonishing Him by saying, "At the very least, you could have been *awake*. That would have been helpful!" But as was usually the case, Jesus didn't just look at the immediate need. He wanted to go deeper. Imagine him exclaiming, "Man, that was a close one!" or "Wow, can you guys believe we made it?" Nope. Instead, Jesus asks a question that still challenges His followers to this day: "Where is your faith?"

I find it interesting that Matthew records Jesus asking this question before He calmed the storm. Matthew 8:26 tells us:

> "He replied, 'You of little faith, why are you so afraid?' Then He got up and rebuked the winds and the waves, and it was completely calm."

It was while the storm was still raging when He wanted to know where their faith was—not after. Sometimes I think Jesus' timing wasn't always the best. He wasn't the most tactful guy around. Wouldn't it have made better sense to calm the storm and then ask serious questions? Yes, but instead He asks them about their faith while the storm is raging. He wants to know if they trust Him while they're in it. When the outcome is uncertain, will they trust Him? When they have tried everything humanly possible, will they trust Him? When it seems as if all hope is lost, will they trust Him?

Where is your faith? This is a simple but loaded question we have all dwelled upon from time to time. Even the most battle-hardened atheist has asked the question, "Do I really *not* believe?" We ask this question because our belief in something matters. What you believe, what I believe, what we place our faith in, is oftentimes set against the backdrop of the trials of life.

I know many of you right now are in a storm. Your faith and beliefs are being challenged. The faith you have always held onto and never wavered from is being confronted. Your wife has informed you she wants a divorce, or you've been laid off from a job you've relied on to pay the bills. Maybe you have just heard the words, "It's terminal." The storm you are facing is unlike any you have ever faced before, and you are left asking yourself the question, "Where is my faith?"

Maybe you are someone who has had faith for decades, or perhaps you've never had faith before. Whatever your situation, you are left dazed, confused, and you wonder if what you really believe is true. Will the belief you have had for so many years see you through the ordeal you are now facing? Everything is so up in the air and you are left to wonder how you can even go on with this storm-tossed life. Because of what you are dealing with, you are definitely at a crossroads now—in your life and faith.

We sat across from each other over a coffee at the Bi-Partisan Café in Portland, Oregon. Bi-Partisan is a popular coffee shop on the east side of Portland, in the Montavilla District. This morning, the café had its regular crowd—a mix of college students studying and business folks meeting. The café displays political artwork on its walls to include representations of every American president. Although the artwork displayed is bipartisan, my friend certainly wasn't. Today, we didn't meet to discuss politics, however. Instead, we discussed theology. He was a boyfriend of one of my wife's co-workers and had a chip on his shoulder toward God and Christians, in particular; this is a typical sentiment in Portland. He was just the kind of person I was looking to interview as part of a class I was taking at a local seminary. It was meant to be an open-ended conversation regarding his thoughts on God, the Bible and Christianity.

As we settled into our seats, I threw out my first question asking him his thoughts about the Bible. Not exactly an easy question to respond to, and his response was both honest and stunning. He said, "I've read the Bible and I know everything about it." I fought the urge to push myself back from the table upon hearing this statement, but I remained engaged while thinking, "Oh, that's interesting coming from a guy who is all of twenty-five years."

After listening to him elaborate more, I asked him about his thoughts on God. He said that "God strikes me as a schizophrenic maniac; happy one minute, and spiteful and vindictive the next." A fair response for sure, as I shared with him that although I never thought of God in quite those terms, I could understand where he was coming from. After all, God did "smite" quite a few people throughout the Old Testament.

As we continued to talk about a wide range of topics, including his own broken childhood and painful church memories, he concluded our time together by saying that, "I just have a hard time believing all of this stuff." While I appreciated his honesty and willingness to share, I was struck by several things during our hour-long interaction.

First, the arrogance and ignorance he displayed was astounding. He exhibited the same undisciplined take on God I have heard from other non-believers. A lazy approach lacking the resolve to dive deeper into the nuances of who God is and what the Bible says. He constantly fell back on the same old boorish atheistic standards of "Christians are stupid," "Pastors just want your money" and "the Church is a crutch."

Despite the criticism he threw my way, I did appreciate his transparency in sharing exactly how he felt. It would have been easy for him to have softened his answers, but he didn't. Also, he showed a complete ignorance regarding Scripture. His struggles with it, though honest, were of the variety of someone who made a quick pass through the text and had not thought things out very well.

Probably the biggest thing that stood out to me was his total lack of faith. His lack of faith wasn't just in Christianity, but our political system, our education system, law enforcement, you name it—he just didn't put much faith into the things of either God or man. As we parted ways, I think he left having felt good about getting stuff off his chest, especially knowing he was talking with a Christian. And I felt good in having heard his perspective on how many people feel about Christianity and God.

Although most people have some sort of a belief in a god and don't necessarily adhere to an atheistic outlook on life, a lot of people can identify with my friend. Most people in America have a sense of what God is about. They have an elementary approach to the Bible, and a surprising number of Americans still read their Bibles on a regular basis.[1] Many have read or heard the classic stories of Moses and the burning bush, or David challenging the giant Goliath, and everyone's favorite, Jonah in the "whale."

Most Americans are aware of who Jesus was. Even if they don't believe that He is the Son of God, they do believe that He was a good man whose teachings can still be applied to our lives today. However, I don't think most would agree with my friend, that they "know everything about Scripture." Most people would probably admit to being ignorant of what the Bible is about. They would agree with him in saying a lot of the stories found throughout Scripture are simply hard to believe. I agree with them!

Talking donkeys[2], people being taken up to heaven without dying[3] and living inside a fish for three days[4]. These stories can try even those with the greatest amount of faith in God. Examples like these and countless others throughout Scripture all require, well…faith. There are two reasons for this.

The first is simply the fact that we weren't there to verify with our own eyes that these events happened. In reading Scripture, Christ followers are being asked to believe in texts that are thousands of years old. And secondly, these events are just hard to believe. How does someone not die and yet be taken up to heaven? How does a guy live in the belly of a great fish for three days? How does a dead man come back to life again? These are the kinds of stories that tripped up my friend at the coffee shop and kept him from coming to a belief in God. If God wasn't in the story, I wouldn't believe them either.

I know this is the kind of material that keeps many people from coming to believe the words of Scripture; it's just too unbelievable. They come to categorize biblical stories as mythology at worst, and at best, they are great stories meant to get across a particular point or truth. In short, many people just can't stomach the stories of Scripture because they require faith; that is, believing in something they have never seen.

We don't know who authored the book of Hebrews. But in the eleventh chapter, the writer asks the question, "What is faith?" This is an important question man has pondered much throughout the course of history. The writer answers by telling us that faith is "confidence in what we hope for and assurance about what we do not see." I don't know about you, but I give a great deal of credibility to things I can see. If I can see it, smell it, touch it, feel it or hear it, I'm good—I believe! Things that I can't perceive with my senses, not so much. So how exactly does one go about having confidence in things we can't see? How does one wrestle with both the seen and the unseen?

The thing about faith is that even though a person has seen God come through before in his or her life, it can still be a challenge to exercise faith in whatever God has next for that person. An example is found with Moses and his encounter with a speaking bush that would not burn up. This was an "a-ha" moment if there ever was one. Witnessing this incredible spectacle should have made it easy for Moses to do whatever the voice asked him to do going forward. But what happened? Moses had a hard time stepping out in faith. Afterwards, in fact multiple times, he complained to God whenever God told him to go to Pharaoh to ask him for permission to go out into the wilderness to worship God. He even went so far as to tell God to go and find someone else. Even though Moses had been hand-picked by God himself to lead the Israelites, he obviously had a hard time putting faith into practice.

The writer of Hebrews goes on to give various examples of what faith looks like. There is the belief in a Creator—something doesn't come from nothing unless there is a designer behind it. There is the pure heart of Abel, the pure life of Enoch, the obedient hearts of Noah and Abraham. He goes on to remind us:

"All these people were still living by faith when they died. They did not receive the things promised; they only saw them and welcomed them from a distance.[5]"

I have a hard time swallowing one big truth from this

passage—if I step out in obedience and exercise my faith, I may never see the results of it. That doesn't seem right to me. After all, I am the one who is taking the risk. I am the one exercising the faith here. I'm the one who's giving the money to that overseas mission organization. I'm the one who volunteers every Sunday in the church pre-school. I'm the one who made a vow to my spouse. In each of these situations and countless others, we don't know the outcome. But faith, true faith, isn't predicated on the outcome.

Faith is all about movement—from doing nothing to doing something. Mission organizations might abuse my money, but I give out of faith. The kid who I faithfully shared Jesus with can follow a different path in life, but in faith, I teach. And my spouse who I vowed to love "till death do us part" can be unfaithful, but I say "I do" in faith. All these situations and countless others require us to step out in faith and practice the confidence in what we hope for.

I mentioned earlier my friend Susan whose husband had fallen and hit his head hard on a concrete floor. Early in his recovery, his situation was looking dire. He was moved out of the hospital and into a long-term treatment facility and was showing no real signs of improvement. He couldn't respond to any stimuli except pain; he wasn't responding to voices, just nothing. And yet Susan wasn't giving up. She had faith that, at the very least, he would eventually show some signs he is in there and aware of his surroundings. She would admit that at this point in the recovery process, her faith was very much being tested. But she continued to hold on to the belief that his situation would improve.

That's the confounding thing about faith. We won't always see the fruits of it! Susan's husband Rick may never regain any semblance of the person he once was. Just like the patriarch Abraham, who was considered righteous because of his faith, so also is Susan proving her faith in *believing* that her husband will get better, not because of the final outcome, whatever that might be, but simply because of her stepping out in faith.

As the storm raged around them, the disciples were at a crossroads. Do they continue to fight the storm in their own strength? Or do they plead with Jesus to do *something*? They knew the situation they were facing was beyond their control. They absolutely needed the supernatural to occur. Even their best efforts in fighting the storm were proving too much for them. They needed Jesus to intercede on their behalf. They needed Jesus to act!

Perhaps this is where you are in your situation. What you are facing is simply too powerful for you to handle anymore. You are tired and worn out and ready to face the One who is all-powerful, all-knowing. The One who loves you beyond measure, and wants to give you His peace, His strength, and remind you that He is with you on this journey.

Questions for Discussion

1. What are some things in the Bible that are just hard to believe?
2. Is faith easy or difficult for you? Explain.
3. Share a time where you just knew something was going to happen, but there was no evidence it would.
4. In what area in your life do you need to step out in faith?

CHAPTER 7

A STEP OF FAITH

"Then he got up and rebuked the winds and the waves, and it
was completely calm."
—Matthew 8:26b

Stepping out is a good term to use when it comes to
faith because when one steps forward there is an
implied action; you are stepping, moving, going in a direction.
Momentum is happening. Author and pastor Mark Batterson
says, "Faith is taking the first step, so that God can take the
next."

Faith is an action word. There is movement when it is put
to use. Two aspects of this part of the Matthew passage
illustrate this. The first is that Jesus got up. But even before
that, He had to wake up. He was roused from His slumber and
saw the need of His friends as they came and begged Him for

help. Because of their petitions, He was moved to act. The next thing He did was to stand up and rebuke the storm. All of this required action on Jesus' part. And because He acted, calm came over the sea, as well as the hearts and minds of His friends.

As I mentioned earlier, in the Army I decided I wanted to pursue being in an Airborne unit. I think you would agree with me that it takes a great deal of faith to take the next step and jump out of a perfectly good airplane. Prior to jumping, you are packed into an aircraft with a couple hundred other jumpers. You have all this gear on, and it's pretty hot and miserable. Finally, after about an hour of flying around, the jumpmaster says, "Stand up!" At this point, you know that the drop zone is near. You are then led through various equipment checks, which is a really good thing. And finally, the side doors of the aircraft open, the drop zone comes into view and the jumpmaster says to the first guy in line, "Stand in the door."

Countless prayers are raised as the green light comes on, testing the paratrooper's faith. All his prior training and confidence comes down to this next step. Does he really believe his parachute will open? Is he ready to apply all he has learned and put it into practice? A paratrooper thinks about a lot of things prior to exiting the aircraft. The battle waged in his head could be summarized by Dr. Dan Allender, who says:

CHRIST IN THE STORM

"The known is a safer enemy than the unknown. Yet we were made for the unknown and to risk danger.[1]"

It would be so much easier to just stay in the aircraft. But where is the fun in that? And more importantly, paratroopers can't fulfill their mission by staying in the plane. And neither can you as a follower of Jesus Christ. Although it is safer, more convenient and comfortable to just stay where we are, Jesus is always calling us forward. This dilemma represents the reason most of us have a problem with faith.

The problem with faith is, it is usually accompanied by its close cousin, fear. It seems as if the two can't live without one another. In fact, I would venture to say that it's not really faith if you have no fear. After all, why do you need faith if you have it all figured out? Why is fear even present? It's because when faith is involved, there is a certain amount of risk. The risk of trying and failing is what keeps many people in their comfort zone. And it's the presence of risk that leads to fear.

I must admit that I am much better at, and have much more practice with, being fearful than I do in having faith of any kind. Fear I know well. Faith, not so much. The truth is I am not much different from the disciples in the storm; I often have too little faith and too much fear. When faced with difficult circumstances, like the disciples at the front of the boat in Rembrandt's painting, I usually rely on my own strength to get me through hard times.

Admittedly, faith is one of those hard to define things in

our world. What is it exactly? As believers in Christ, we are told we should do everything in faith. So, does that mean we just trudge forward without giving thought to the implications of our actions? Of course not. Faith must always have a reason for going forward. When Jesus said to His disciples, "Let us go over to the other side of the lake," do you wonder as I do, if Jesus took His disciples to the other side of the lake as a way of stretching their faith and showing them, He was God? Did Jesus know they were going to face a storm before they ventured out? Did Jesus know they were going to face a demoniac when they landed on the other side of the lake? If we believe that God is all-knowing, then the answer is obvious —of course He knew.

I am convinced that up until their sail around the lake, the disciples did not fully believe that Jesus was God. If they did, they would have been sleeping alongside Him when the storm arose; they would not have given much attention to the wind and rain that was buffeting their tiny vessel. Instead, they would have had full trust and confidence that Jesus would not allow for them to drown while He was present. This storm, however, was a trial Jesus knew His followers needed to go through to increase their faith in Him.

This, of course, begs the question, is that the same for us today? Does God allow trials to come our way so that our faith in God can increase? Does our faith in God only increase through trials? I hate to say it, but I think so. There is complexity in that statement, isn't there? The alternative is if a person doesn't go through a trial, does that mean they can't be drawn closer to God? I don't believe so. But one cannot argue with the fact that God, throughout the course of history, has used trials to repeatedly increase the faith of His followers. Why? I think it's because as people, we thrive when we face difficulties. Challenges in life cause us to look outside of ourselves to something bigger—they cause us to look up.

I also believe there is something in each of us that will rise to the occasion when facing the challenge before us. Without a challenge, most of us would stay right where we are, growing more and more complacent or apathetic in our relationship with God until He wakes us up, through difficulty, into a new-found level of faith in Him.

It's like an athlete who prepares to compete at the highest level, and must be challenged along the way. Even being challenged by his fellow teammates is not quite the same as entering the arena of competition against an unfamiliar foe. It is only in this arena that he gains a true measure of his talents and level of preparedness. And, so it is with faith. It's easy to say, "I have faith," but faith must be tested to discover how true and genuine it really is. As famous British author, C.S. Lewis, once noted:

"God has not been trying an experiment on my faith or love in order to find out their quality. He knew it already. It was I who didn't. In this trial He makes us occupy the dock, the witness box, and the bench all at once. He always knew that my temple was a house of cards. His only way of making me realize the fact was to knock it down.[2]"

Faith is only made true when it is tested by the storms of life, when we are challenged beyond our own efforts. In the movie *The Last Crusade*, explorer Indiana Jones had to pass three tests on his search for the Holy Grail. One of those tests was to cross the "Path of God," an invisible foot bridge that spanned a deep chasm. Tension hangs in the air as Indy is pinned against a cliff overlooking the wide gulf between where he is and where he wants to go. He knows intellectually, according to his father's notes, there is a bridge right in front of him. The problem is he is unable to physically see it until he steps out in faith.

After some tense moments, Indy eventually takes that all important first step and successfully walks across the bridge. He finds the Holy Grail, saves his father's life, and in the end, rides off into the sunset. But the first thing he had to do was to risk everything and take that first step out in faith, believing in that which he could not see.

First steps are always the most difficult, but they set into motion an opportunity for God to act. A wonderful example of faith occurred in the life of a young girl named Esther, a teenager who was thrust into a position she didn't ask for and given a responsibility she wasn't ready for. An edict had been issued unwittingly by the king to kill every Jew throughout the land of Persia. With her people on the verge of genocide, her cousin Mordecai petitioned her to save him, her and the Jewish people.

> "For if you remain silent at this time, relief and deliverance for the Jews will arise from another place, but you and your father's family will perish. And who knows but that you have come to your royal position for such a time as this?[3]"

With so much at stake, Esther had a choice to make— approach the king uninvited and risk death, or remain silent and her people perish? She understood anyone visiting the king without an invitation put their life in peril. Despite this, Esther stepped out in faith and placed her life on the line. She overcame her fear and approached the king to tell him about the sinister plot of the evil villain, Haman.

We know the end of the story. Esther was obedient to the cause, and she saved the lives of her people. To commemorate her heroic act of faith, Jews around the world still remember her by observing Purim. Her story, and many other examples, show us obedience isn't simply an act we blindly go into. Instead, her example shows us how we must take action at times because there is much at stake.

Perhaps, like Esther, the challenge you are currently facing is too big. Perhaps there is too much for you to risk if you were to step out in faith. You might even be thinking there is no way this thing can happen—the situation you are in is impossible. Batterson again reminds us:

> "Impossible odds set the stage for God's greatest miracles.[4]"

I am aware many of you need a miracle, as the storm you are currently facing is unlike any you have ever faced before. You don't see an end to it, and you definitely can't see how this particular trial can be any good whatsoever. You are exhausted and your faith in God is waning. When faced with trials, many people simply give up on God and follow the old adage, how can a good God allow for this to happen? It goes back to the question, "Where is your faith?" I know this is a question I have pondered a lot in my life.

My friend, Emily, has a daughter who has suffered from terrible seizures her entire life. Her daughter has been life-flighted to Denver hospitals numerous times due to the twenty-minute-long seizures that have at times, even stopped her breathing. This has been a long, six-year storm for Emily and her family. As if that isn't challenging enough, Emily herself was just recently diagnosed with two different tumors that if surgically removed will greatly affect her ability to care for her daughter.

I recently asked her, *how do you keep your faith? What keeps you from giving up?* She said, "I don't know what I would do without God in our lives." She went on to tell me that this ordeal has made her faith in God stronger than ever. She can't imagine how people face trials without God in their lives.

Emily wouldn't admit this, but I think she is a true hero of the faith. If it were me, I would be railing against God, "Why me, Lord? Why are You allowing this to happen? What did I do wrong?" Emily prays that God will heal her daughter. But she also is at a point in her faith where she understands that this years-long ordeal may not just be about healing. Instead, Emily sees how her daughter's illness is shaping her to be more like Christ.

She has become more understanding, selfless, and patient during her daughter's illness. She has seen firsthand how Jesus shows up for her and her family through the hands and feet of her community. Emily has come to an understanding that Jesus is in the boat with her regardless of the outcome. I love what Pastor Greg Laurie says to encourage us whenever we are going through trouble:

"Maybe you're in the midst of a storm right now. God has allowed it to make you more like Jesus.[5]"

This was certainly the case for Emily. What Jesus illustrated for His followers was that He was right there with them during a very difficult time. And in the same way, He is with us. So knowing that, what area in your life do you need to say, "You know what? Forget it...I'm just going to do it?"

Whatever *it* is, are you willing to take the first step and pursue the dream you have been putting off? Maybe you have been sitting on a decision for a long time and now is the time to decide. Now is the time for action, now is the time for you to step out in faith. Be mindful of what the ancient prophet Isaiah told the nation Israel:

> "Do not fear, for I have redeemed you;
>   I have called you by name; you are Mine![6]"

Knowing God is with you provides the confidence to step out in faith, which is an act of worship, as we'll see in the next chapter.

Questions for Discussion

1. Is it easy or difficult for you to practice faith?
2. Who is someone you know who practices faith?
3. Have difficult circumstances increased or decreased your faith in God?

CHAPTER 8

WORSHIP

"The men were amazed and asked, 'What kind of man is this?
Even the winds and the waves obey him!'"
—Matthew 8:27

*O*ur story began with a tale about the loss of a five-hundred-year-old rare work of art stolen from a poorly secured museum in the Fenway–Kenmore neighborhood of Boston, Massachusetts. In the aftermath, the very fabric of the museum and the larger art world was ripped to shreds. Since then, the Gardner has installed state-of-the-art security intended to thwart even the most sophisticated of art thieves. But these efforts of enhanced security rose out of the grief-stricken ashes of loss.

Interestingly, loss in our own lives is the place where true change and true worship begin. It is out of the depths of our souls, when we are taken to our limits and restored, that we truly understand the sense of amazement, bewilderment and awe the disciples felt in that tiny boat on the Sea of Galilee.

Like the Gardner Museum, the disciples had something stolen from them, also. Their peace and security were taken and replaced by unsettling fear. When they were most vulnerable, out on the open water, a storm left them fighting for their lives. You may notice in Rembrandt's painting of the chaotic scene, there are two men whose backs are to us. The gray-haired man in the beige tunic to the left of Rembrandt, and the man with the brown cloak who is kneeling, facing Jesus.

Despite the commotion going on in this scene, both of these men appear to be doing what is most important in a time of peril, which is to come to Jesus in prayer. During the storm, they are doing what we should all do when it seems circumstances are beyond our control. When we have done everything we possibly can, we reach out to God. Prayer, of course, is a form of worship, and these men were worshipping Jesus during their time of need. And I'm sure they most certainly worshipped Jesus again once the storm had subsided and peace was restored.

But what does it mean to worship? The first thing I think of when I hear the word "worship" is music. I immediately think of gathering in church where everyone faces a group of singers and musicians who are leading the congregation in songs of praise. Singing songs of praise is certainly an important aspect of worship, but it is just one piece of what it means to worship God. We can worship God with our money by giving our financial resources to kingdom causes. We can worship God through giving our time by volunteering with organizations that are furthering the Gospel message. Worship, true, heartfelt worship, can only come about when one recognizes, as the disciples did on the lake, their need for a Savior. Pastor John Piper says:

"True worship is based on a right understanding of God's nature, and it is a right valuing of God's worth.[1]"

I admit that I don't always have a right understanding of God. And I certainly don't have a right understanding of God's worth. Grasping who God is doesn't always come easy, does it? Worshipping God also means that we are giving of ourselves which begins at the starting points of humility and confession. First off, in humility, one must come to an admission of who you are before an almighty, holy God. Pastor Timothy Keller says it like this:

"The Christian Gospel is that I am so flawed that Jesus had to die for me, yet I am so loved and valued that Jesus was glad to die for me. This leads to deep humility and deep confidence at the same time. It undermines both swaggering and sniveling. I cannot feel superior to anyone, and yet I have nothing to prove to anyone. I do not think more of myself nor less of myself. Instead, I think of myself less.[2]"

In our world, where we are rewarded for putting ourselves above all others to get ahead, humility is oftentimes absent. But there is no better example of humility than Christ Himself, who took on a human form and died a criminal's death. In doing this, He displayed the greatest degree of humility. Paul reminds the church of Philippi that Christ:

"...who, although He existed in the form of God, did not regard equality with God a thing to be grasped...[3]"

Jesus gave us a model to follow with this act of humility.

The second part of worship is confession—confessing that one is a sinner in need of a Savior. This is when one comes to the realization that Jesus is the Lord and Master of all. I have always wondered what does "Lord" mean? I mean "Lord" is such an old term, right? The dictionary defines "Lord" as "One having power and authority over others.[4]"

We're probably more familiar with this term being used in British aristocratic society. If you have ever read *Pride and Prejudice* or *Sense and Sensibility* or any other work by Jane Austen, you are familiar with that term. It was a common term used by those who leased land or other property to an individual or many individuals. Think of a landlord. Scripturally speaking, when you are reading your Bible and you see the word "LORD" in capital letters, that is in reference to the covenant name of God, YAHWEH, and the position of YAHWEH to His people. It was a straightforward way of saying, "Our God is our Master."

In the New Testament, the term "Lord" is the most frequently used title for Jesus Christ. It's an acknowledgment of Jesus' position as Master of our lives. But we don't typically like the idea of anyone being a Master over us, do we? British poet William Ernest Henley, said:

"I am the master of my fate; I am the captain of my soul.[5]"

That kind of thinking resonates more with our independent spirit. Like Adam and Eve, we tend to think our way is the best way. We tend to take the Word of God as a collection of suggestions. More often than not, as we build our own little kingdoms of which we are the "master," we get ourselves in trouble, don't we? I think to a certain degree we all struggle with allowing Jesus to be the Master or Lord over our lives. I know I do. Although we have a desire to follow the ways of God, we also feel the compelling tug of the things in our world.

In the late 70s, singer and songwriter Bob Dylan had a profound spiritual experience in a hotel room in Arizona. This experience led him to embrace Christianity.

"Jesus did appear to me as King of Kings, and Lord of Lords! There was a presence in the room that couldn't have been anybody but Jesus... Jesus put his hand on me. It was a physical thing. I felt it. I felt it all over me. I felt my whole body tremble. The glory of the Lord knocked me down and picked me up.[6]"

I think we would all agree that's quite a conversion experience, isn't it? The first album he recorded after coming to faith was one titled "Slow Train Coming." In the album, he recorded a song called, "Gotta Serve Somebody." Most people recognize Bob Dylan as an icon in American pop culture. In the song, Dylan says we all have a choice as to whom we are going to serve. He is making a point that we all serve somebody or something.

We all have a Master whom we serve. So, the question for us is, "Do we make Jesus 'Lord' of our lives?" This is the challenge for all of us, isn't it? This is what "sanctification" looks like; sanctification is a churchy word that simply means *becoming more Christlike*. It's the giving up of those areas of our lives where we have been Master—where we have been in control—and giving Jesus control. It is confessing that Jesus is Master and Lord.

A great example of this happened to Peter, one of Jesus' closest followers. Matthew captures an interesting interaction between Jesus and His friends.

Located one hundred fifty miles north of Jerusalem, the

mostly Gentile region of Caesarea Philippi sat at the base of Mount Hermon where it was one of the sources of the Jordan River. The region was fertile with green trees and grass. Because of this, it became a center of pagan worship in the region. The Canaanite god of good fortune was worshipped there. Pan, the flute playing half-man, half-goat god of fright, where we get the word "panic," was worshipped there.

There was a grotto or a cave that had water flowing from it, into which residents would throw sacrifices as a way of worshipping Pan. Herod the Great, who was the ruler when Christ was born, built a temple there to honor Caesar Augustus.

With this as the backdrop Jesus wanted to know what the word on the street was about Him and asked his followers:

"Who do people say the Son of Man is?"

They replied, "Some say John the Baptist; others say Elijah; and still others, Jeremiah or one of the prophets."

"But what about you?" He asked. "Who do you say I am?"

Simon Peter answered, "You are the Messiah, the Son of the living God."

Jesus replied, "Blessed are you, Simon son of Jonah, for this was not revealed to you by flesh and blood, but by My Father in heaven.[7]"

It's helpful to understand the context in which Jesus asks this question. First of all, by the time Jesus asks this question, He had already performed numerous healings. He had already fed the crowd of five thousand and his friends had been eyewitnesses to the miraculous. The second thing to help us understand the context is that Caesarea Philippi was mostly a Gentile region.

Peter offers us what was probably the first creed or confession of faith. "You are the Christ, the Son of the living God." By way of this admittance, Peter was worshipping the Lord in all truth.

Confessing also involves admitting our shortcomings, which isn't a popular thing to do, is it? After all, when a person confesses to wrongdoing, they are opening themselves to others. They become vulnerable and at the mercy of the person to whom they are confessing. As difficult as confession is, it is an important aspect of our faith. Confessing our sins before God acts as a purifying agent for the soul. It's a means of removing a heavy weight—a burden in our lives we were never meant to carry. In humility, we are admitting our shortcomings before a perfect God. Job understood this type of humility when he declared:

"My ears had heard of you
    but now my eyes have seen you.
    Therefore I despise myself
    and repent in dust and ashes.[8]"

Job confessed that his knowledge of the created order of the world was limited, and that God, as the Creator, is all-knowing and all-sufficient.

From our Matthew 8 passage, we learn it was the challenge of the storm that brought the disciples to a closer relationship and a better understanding of who Jesus was. When Jesus cried out, "Peace be still!" it was a command that resonated beyond the clouds and raindrops of that time and speaks to the storms we face today. The clouds parted, the rain stopped, the thunder and lightning ceased and the water returned to a gentle calmness.

The disciples were amazed at what they had just witnessed, and with water still dripping from their faces, they asked the question, "What kind of man is this? Even the winds and the waves obey Him!" A question asked even though they had witnessed Jesus heal the sick, relieve the possessed from their demons and renew the leper's skin. It wasn't until they witnessed Jesus' command over the very forces of nature *and* through saving their own lives that they came to the realization that Jesus was God. This challenge on the sea was a turning point in how they viewed Jesus.

Like the disciples in the boat, we read about many others in Scripture who came face-to-face with Jesus and their lives were radically changed after their encounter with Him. Saul became Paul. Zacchaeus went from a notorious tax collector to a philanthropic community leader. Peter went from a scared, arrogant know-it-all to the person on whom the Church would be built. The transformation that Peter experienced is the same that billions of people throughout history have experienced. People's lives have been radically changed because they encountered and worshipped Jesus Christ of Nazareth.

The story of the stolen Gardner paintings is not complete. Their empty frames still hang on the walls waiting to once again be filled with their priceless art. And your story isn't finished either. God has always been passionately in love with you. From the beginning of time, God has been our pursuer. And he is pursuing you today. No matter where you are in your journey with Jesus, He is calling unto you as a Bridegroom calls unto his Bride.

Is this the year you step out in faith and face your fears knowing that Jesus will face them with you? Is now the time where, in your moment of desperation, you reach out to Jesus? Let this be the year where you live with abandon and worship Jesus as your Lord and Savior.

Questions for Discussion

1. Does worshipping God come easy for you, or is it more difficult?
2. Would you say Jesus is Lord of your life?
3. Who is the most humble person you have ever known?
4. Is confession to God and to others a regular part of your walk with God?

CONCLUSION

Rembrandt's painting represents a moment in time in the lives of the disciples. It captures the tumultuous tempest they faced, the chaotic struggle to maintain control and, ultimately, their willingness to turn to Jesus.

It demonstrates those things that are so often threatened to be taken from us; an unclear view of life, security, confidence in our own strength, and most importantly, the threat of losing our peace and hope. The painting illustrates the seemingly chaotic disorder of our world and the randomness of how things play out.

Christ in the Storm on the Sea of Galilee and the other stolen rare works of art are still missing, only empty frames remain hanging at the Gardner. There have been reported sightings of the artwork over the years in places like Connecticut, Pennsylvania, Ireland and even a darkened warehouse. The artwork supposedly has been in the hands of the Boston Mafia and the Irish Republican Army. Unfortunately, many of the people who were allegedly involved with the theft are now dead, and whoever has the paintings hasn't been persuaded to claim the $10 million reward money the museum is offering for their return.

The absence of the paintings presents an obvious tension, doesn't it? No one knows when or if they will ever be returned. And this is a tension indicative of the struggles we face in our own lives. It would be nice to put a tidy bow on the case of the stolen art and know they have been put back in their rightful place at the Gardner. It would also be nice to have a happy ending to the struggle you are currently facing.

Fortunately, the Rembrandt painting doesn't tell the whole story. If Rembrandt would have created another scene, one immediately following Jesus' waking, he would have shown the hands that were so fervently struggling to steer the rudder are now outstretched towards the one who steers our lives. The man who was cowering in fear, hands clenched, because of indecision or inability, now with confidence restored, has his arms wrapped around Jesus in utter gratitude and exultation. The old man whose back was turned to Jesus, perhaps as a resignation to his own fate during the storm, or because of past sins, is now facing Jesus with the look of new life upon his face. And those who were closest to Jesus praying, begging, and angry with Him are now reverently bowed, face down, in worship of the One who calms storms.

And finally, Rembrandt would have painted Jesus standing with outstretched arms facing a bright shining sun. The sea would be as calm as glass, and the disciples, though bent over from exhaustion, would be worshiping Jesus in awe of what had just transpired.

Although the outcome of your predicament might be uncertain, one thing you can be certain of is Jesus' presence in the challenge you are facing. I encourage you to continue to press on in your struggle, and in the words of an old childhood friend of mine, Pastor Charlie Marque:

"When life is confusing—even disappointing—and next steps are hard to determine, we can heed the words of the great apostle Paul and do one thing, press on toward Jesus."

A great reminder for all of us is to focus our sights on Jesus for the faith we need today.

And that's the beauty of the story. Christ in the Storm on the Sea of Galilee is ultimately a story that ends with peace, hope and joy restored. There is peace in knowing that God, who desperately loves you, is with you in the storms of life. The empty frames in the Gardner represent hope; hope that one day the stolen art will be returned to their rightful owner. But also hope in knowing that any pains we face in this life will give way to heavenly delight in the next. And finally, joy in knowing that the broken relationship between God and man has been restored in the person of Jesus Christ.

May this painting be a visual reminder to you to not give up and continue moving forward in the faith and knowledge of Jesus Christ.

Anyone with information on the stolen art should contact Director of Security by phone at 617-278-5114 or by email at theft@gardnermuseum.org.

NOTES

COPYRIGHT

1. Version 1.0 08.27.2021

INTRODUCTION

1. https://www.patheos.com/resources/additional-resources/2009/07/praying-with-art-visio-divina. Accessed December 6, 2018.

CHAPTER 1

1. Romans 5:5 NASB
2. Matthew 26:31–35
3. Matthew 26:69-75
4. Manning, Brennan, *The Ragamuffin Gospel* (Sisters: Multnomah, 1990), 20.
5. 2 Corinthians 3:5
6. Charles R. Swindoll, *Getting Through the Tough Stuff: It's Always Something!* (Nashville: W Publishing Group, 2004), 176, 185
7. John 21:15–17

CHAPTER 2

1. Final straggler: the Japanese soldier who outlasted Hiroo Onoda, www.mikedashhistory.com. Accessed, December 7, 2017.
2. Genesis 12:1, 4
3. Genesis 6:14
4. Jonah 3:3

5. 1 Samuel 15:22
6. James 1:22

CHAPTER 3

1. Mark 4:37.
2. Genesis 3
3. Lewis, C. S. *The Problem of Pain* (1940; repr., San Francisco: HarperSanFrancisco, 2001), 91.
4. James 1:2–4
5. John 9:1–3
6. The Bible Exposition Commentary New Testament, Vol. 1 © 2003 by Warren W. Wiersbe. Used by permission of David C Cook. May not be further reproduced. All rights reserved.
7. Psalm 46:7, 11
8. Arthur Jackson, *Our Daily Bread*, "Present in the Storm, June 20." https://odb.org/2019/06/20/present-in-the-storm. Accessed June 28, 2019.

CHAPTER 4

1. Wilgers, Christopher, *Break Free!* (Bloomington: WestBow Press, 2014), 1.
2. Lore: Episode 2, The Bloody Pit. March 22, 2015. Listened to on Jan. 18, 2019
3. CaringBridge journal entry of my friend in Texas, Susan Feldmiller.

CHAPTER 5

1. Matthew 9:21
2. Luke 8:47-48
3. https://www.southeastchristian.org/sermons/the-gift-of-desperation/. Listened to on October 3, 2018

CHAPTER 6

1. (The State of the Bible; 6 Trends for 2014, 2018) https://www.barna.com/research/the-state-of-the-bible-6-trends-for-2014/
2. Numbers 22:21–41
3. Genesis 5:21–24 , 2 Kings 2:11.
4. Jonah 1:17
5. Hebrews 11:13a

CHAPTER 7

1. Allender, Dan, *The Wounded Heart* (Carol Stream, NavPress, 1990), 46.
2. Lewis, C. S., *A Grief Observed,* (Faber and Faber, 1961), 26.
3. Esther 4:14
4. The Ripple Effect | Chase the Lion | Media | National Community Church. Listened to on April 13, 2021.
5. Smoke Signals to Heaven (harvest.org)
6. Isaiah 43:1 NASB.

CHAPTER 8

1. Piper, John, https://www.desiringgod.org/interviews/what-is-worship, accessed on 1/14/19.
2. Keller, Timothy, *"The Reason for God: Belief in an Age of Skepticism"* (New York: Penguin Random House, 2008), 187.
3. Philippians 2:6 NASB.
4. Mirriam-Webster.com, Accessed on February 16, 2019.
5. Henley, William Ernest, *A Book of Verses,* (Nabu Press, 1897), 56–57
6. Heylin, Clinton, *Bob Dylan: Behind the Shades Revisited,* (New York, HarperCollins, 1991), 491.
7. Matthew 16:13b–17.
8. Job 42:5-6.

Made in the USA
Monee, IL
06 September 2021